COLLECTED POEMS
OF
DENIS DEVLIN

DENIS DEVLIN IN WASHINGTON

COLLECTED POEMS OF DENIS DEVLIN

EDITED BY J. C. C. MAYS

WAKE FOREST UNIVERSITY PRESS

WAKE FOREST UNIVERSITY PRESS
Box 7333 Winston-Salem, North Carolina 27109

ISBN 0-916390-37-3

Originated by
The Dedalus Press,
24 The Heath, Cypress Downs, Dublin 6W, Ireland.

Designed by Raymond Kyne Associates, Dublin.
Typeset and Printed by The Nationalist, Carlow.

Congratulations on your edition
of Denis Devlin's "Collected Poems".
Amends at last.

Samuel Beckett

PREFACE

The present volume brings together the poems and translations Denis Devlin published during his lifetime. It constitutes a representative body of work, and the one on which his reputation will rest.

It is arranged round his three major collections — two which he oversaw and a third he did not live to complete. There is some overlapping between the first two, *Intercessions* and *Lough Derg*, which is justified because the organisation of each volume comprises a statement in its entirety and because of the interest afforded by the revisions. Even when the revisions are not extensive, or have only to do with punctuation, their overall effect is no less significant.

The section representing Devlin's third collection is organised according to the sequence in which its parts were published in journals. It is likely other poems would have been added, that the composition of the whole would have changed, and that revisions would have been made as the enterprise proceeded. The poems and translations Devlin published but did not collect are grouped together following each of the major collections.

The other features of the present volume should be made clear at the outset. First, despite its title, it does not include a number of poems to be found in previous collections by Allen Tate and Robert Penn Warren (1963) and Brian Coffey (1964), or which have been published subsequently in magazines like *The Lace Curtain*. The explanation is that another, separate volume is planned which will contain the poems and translations Devlin did not publish during his lifetime.

The unpublished material that has been made available has been of interest and frequently of value. It nonetheless constitutes a somewhat piecemeal selection, and a stage has been reached when the order and relative status of all the material together must be established before continuing. The present volume can be considered in the same light as the *Collected Poems* of Wallace Stevens. It will be supplemented in time by a further volume of *Opus Posthumous*.

The other word of caution concerns the notes, which are deliberately sparing, and more concerned with textual matters than with elucidation and commentary. Devlin's habit was to preserve everything he wrote, and to return to revise at intervals in ways that often modified the original inspiration and sometimes overtook it. Again, his kind of commitment to poetry involved him and involves his readers in processes which are difficult to terminate, and a full display of variants and alternatives and rejected passages would display such a feature more accurately than the appearance of a single, final text.

The present volume is in this respect far from being a full record of Devlin's published poems. He left behind superceded versions and rejected sections, as well as a large number of drafts and revised fair copies of nearly every title included here. If they had been incorporated, the volume would have been twice as bulky, and its nature would be different. Separate editions of longer poems like *Est Prodest* and *The Passion of Christ*, on the model of Brian Coffey's edition of *The Heavenly Foreigner*, would repair a deficiency of which I am sorely aware.

I should like to thank Brian Coffey and Michael Smith, in particular, among Devlin's previous editors. The magnitude and skill of Brian Coffey's work will be appreciated by anyone who attempts to follow him, while Michael Smith has been tireless in preserving the idea of Devlin's poetry among living poets in Ireland. I deeply regret that Niall Montgomery and John Jordan, strong advocates of Devlin's poems, did not live to see this new collection.

I should also like to thank, for particular assistance of different kinds, Catherine Fahy and Brian McKenna of the National Library; Dr Bruce Bradley, SJ, of Belvedere College; Professor Roger Little of Trinity College; Mervyn Wall; Denis Devlin's sisters, Eileen O'Connor, Moya Lindsay, Anne Smyth and Shiela Healy, and his son, Stephen Devlin; Dr Eoghan Ó hAnluain of University College; Raymond Kyne; and the persistent and resourceful publisher of this volume, John F. Deane.

J.C.C. MAYS
University College, Dublin

CONTENTS

INTERCESSIONS (1937)

UNCOLLECTED EARLY POEMS AND TRANSLATIONS

LOUGH DERG AND OTHER POEMS (1946)

Translation of Exile and Other Poems by St-John Perse

Later Poems (1946-1959)

Uncollected Later Poems and Translations

Biographical Note and Editor's Introduction

Denis Devlin: Biographical Note

1908: 15 April, born Greenock, Scotland, of Irish parents, the eldest of nine children.

1920: the family returned to Ireland. DD's father, Liam, a native of Derry, kept licensed premises at 68 Parnell Street, Dublin, which were a frequent meeting place of Michael Collins and his associates during the struggle for independence. The family afterwards moved to a large house, Westbury, in Stillorgan.

At first, DD attended the Christian Brothers' School in Richmond Street.

1923—26: DD attended Belvedere College, where he was contemporary with Mervyn Wall and Niall Montgomery.

He at once established himself academically and socially. He wrote the Cumann na Gaedhilge notes in *The Belvederian* in 1924. In his second year, he became a member of the Debating Society, won the Rector's Prize for an Irish essay entitled ''Oidche i n-Eirinn i n-aimsir Chormaic Mhic Airt'' and was received into the Sodality of the Blessed Virgin Mary. In his final year, he became Sacristan of the BVM Sodality, a school prefect, secretary of the Debating Society and a member of the Irish-speaking Conference of St John Berchmans (St Vincent de Paul Society). He played Banquo in *Macbeth* and M. de la Porcheraie in *Moi* to plaudits, and took first place in French and second in English in the Honours Leaving Certificate for the whole country.

1926—27: after Belvedere, he entered the diocesan seminary, All Hallow's College, Clonliffe, from where he enrolled at University College Dublin with a view to taking a degree in modern languages. He left Clonliffe in 1927.

1927—29: DD's first-year results at UCD gave him a scholarship worth £30, and thereafter he participated widely in undergraduate life. He was contemporary with Mervyn Wall, Niall Montgomery, Brian O'Nolan, Cyril Cusack, Donagh MacDonagh, Niall Sheridan, Brian Coffey.

He became auditor of the Legion Française, secretary of the English Literature Society, a member of the committee of the Literary and Historical (debating) Society, a founder-member and secretary of the Dramatic Society (he played a memorable Feste in *Twelfth Night*).

1928—29: during his final undergraduate year, DD also enrolled as a law student at King's Inns, but he did not sit the First Law examination and did not re-enroll thereafter.

1929: DD was awarded first-class honours in both English and French in the BA examination (with a less-distinguished qualification in Irish), as a result of which he was awarded an exhibition of £20.

1929—30: he continued at UCD, working for an MA in French, by examination and thesis, and for one of three travelling studentships awarded by the National University of Ireland.

January 1930, a poem published in *The National Student* confirmed his reputation among his contemporaries for advanced literary views.

Summer 1930, DD spent the summer in the Blaskets, improving his Irish for the studentship examination. Though he failed to win a studentship (£200 p.a. for two years), he was awarded a special prize of £50 in view of his high standard in French, and he passed the examination component of the MA.

September 1930, *Poems* — with Brian Coffey — published, in an edition of 250 copies with an additional pre-publication reprint of 100 copies, at the authors' own expense.

1930—31: travelled in Europe, studying for part of the time in Munich.

1931: submitted thesis at UCD entitled *Montaigne intime* and awarded MA (second-class honours).

1931—33: continued his studies at the Sorbonne, with the degree of Docteur-en-Lettres in mind. In Paris, he resumed his friendship with Brian Coffey, and, through new friends like Gaston Bonheur, Roger Bullion and Thomas McGreevy, broadened his literary acquaintance.

April 1932, visit to Spain (including visit to Avila) with the American journalist, Sam Pope Brewer.

May 1933, the third number of *14, rue du Dragon* published DD's *Passerelle*, translated into French by Gaston Bonheur.

1933—34: returned to Dublin, without paid employment. ''I can remember many gloomy evenings walking about town, our walk and slow talk interrupted occasionally by Denis pausing beneath a lamppost to draw a scrap of paper from his pocket and read by the light overhead some new poem which he had written.'' (Mervyn Wall)

1934: Samuel Beckett named Brian Coffey and DD as ''without question the most interesting of the youngest generation of Irish poets'' in an article on ''Recent Irish Poetry'' in the August *Bookman*, and quoted from the writing DD had been doing in Paris.

Appointed to one of four newly-created junior positions (Demonstratorships) in the English Department at UCD, at a salary of £150 p.a.

At some point between 1933 and 1936, DD made a tour of cathedral towns in England and Scotland.

1934—38: poems, translations and reviews published in *Contemporary Poetry and Prose, The Dublin Magazine, Ireland Today, transition* and *Thorns of Thunder: Selected Poems of Paul Eluard* ed George Reavey.

1935: resigned from UCD and entered the Department of Foreign Affairs as a cadet, at a salary of £400 p.a. ''I know the academic life is a superior one,'' he told Mervyn Wall, ''but I admit that the diplomatic life attracts me.''

He subsequently became secretary to the Irish Legation that went to negotiate the settlement of the economic war, and he accompanied de Valera to the League of Nations at Geneva and to an eye specialist in Zurich.

1937: DD's collection of fifteen poems, *Intercessions*, published by Europa Press (limited to 300 copies). It was dismissed by *The Criterion* and *The Times Literary Supplement*, but praised highly by Beckett in *transition* and McGreevy in *Ireland Today*.

1938: posted to Rome as first secretary in the legation to Italy. First visit to Greece.

1939: appointed consul at the Consulate General in New York.

In the following half-dozen years, published in a variety of American journals: *Accent, Briarcliff Quarterly, Calendar, Maryland Quarterly, New Republic, Poetry, Sewanee Review, Southern Review, University of Kansas City Review.*

1940: appointed first secretary, legation to Washington.

1945—49: translations from St.-John Perse, whom he met in Washington (*Rains* published 1944 and 1945, *Snows* 1945, *Exile and Other Poems* 1949). Also translations in *Botteghe Oscure* 1952 (René Char), *Briarcliff Quarterly* 1946 (Perse), *Quarterly Review of Literature* 1947 (Valéry) and *The Limits of Art* ed Huntington Cairns 1948 (Verlaine).

1946: married an American of French descent, Marie Caren Radon. Visited Mexico.

Lough Derg and Other Poems published by Reynal and Hitchcock. Widely reviewed, by Babette Deutsch, Dudley Fitts, Randall Jarrell, Richard Lattimore, Arthur Mizener and others.

1947: appointed counsellor in the office of the High Commissioner, London.

1949: appointed counsellor at headquarters in Dublin. *Irish Writing* published part of *The Heavenly Foreigner*; full versions published over the next two years in other Irish and American, Italian and English magazines.

1950: appointed minister plenipotentiary to Italy.

1951: accredited to Turkey as minister plenipotentiary.

1952—59: *The Colours of Love* published in *Botteghe Oscure*, 1952; *Mr. Allen* in *Partisan Review*, 1955; *The Tomb of Michael Collins* in *Sewanee Review*, 1956;

The Passion of Christ in *Encounter*, 1957; *Memoirs of a Turcoman Diplomat* in *Botteghe Oscure*, 1959.

1958: when the Irish legation in Rome was raised to the status of embassy, DD named ambassador to Italy.

1959: 21 August, died from leukaemia at St. Vincent's Nursing Home, Dublin.

1963: *Selected Poems* ed Allen Tate and Robert Penn Warren published by Holt, Rinehart and Winston. Widely reviewed, by Marius Bewley, Hayden Carruth, Howard Moss and others.

The Complete Poems ed Brian Coffey published as a special issue of *University Review* (Dublin) 1963; reissued with additions as *Collected Poems* (The Dolmen Press 1964).

1967: *The Heavenly Foreigner* ed Brian Coffey (Dolmen Editions 1967).

INTRODUCTION

The nineteen-thirties have long possessed a special interest in literary history because they encompass the transition from modernism to late modernism. They have also attracted the attention of those who would recover the different, often stifled beginnings of postmodernism. The period is of interest from a different perspective, from the point of view of the way modernism was modified and resisted and postmodernism was driven underground.

It is helpful to begin with some brief comments on the decade because the reviving interest in Denis Devlin's poems has attached itself to the issues involved. His writing has attracted readers who have taken it to stand for a kind which anticipates the ambitions of writing now, and which is cognate with the beginnings of postmodernism in other traditions. In Ireland, he has been taken as an exemplary poet of a kind at variance with the dominant antimodernist tradition and a kind of rallying-point.

I

An identical, roughly parallel narrative may be traced among the three English traditions of the Atlantic seaboard. In America, while great early moderns like Robert Frost, Marianne Moore, Wallace Stevens and e. e. cummings consolidated their oeuvres, a younger generation — John Crowe Ransom, Allen Tate, Robert Penn Warren — inherited what they understood as a shared, by-then established tradition and developed it differently. The writing of Ezra Pound and William Carlos Williams appeared less central to the time, and the writing of those who continued the alternative Pound-Williams version of modernism — Louis Zukofsky, Lorine Niedecker, George Oppen — was ignored. Only during the years of postmodern reaction was a connection with the alternative version of modernism renewed, and Zukofsky and the others found a widespread readership for the first time.

The situation in Britain in the nineteen-thirties is equivalent, if not the same. T. S. Eliot's writing and concerns ceased to have much relevance to the tradition of modernism he previously helped to establish, and what was vital in his earlier work was taken up and developed differently by the younger, Auden generation. The work of those who did not fall into either camp — for instance, Hugh MacDiarmid and Basil Bunting — was ignored until it was rediscovered in the sixties, when a new kind of modernism looked over the head of the several kinds of writing which had intervened.

In Ireland, the thirties were dominated on the one hand by W. B. Yeats and such later Twilighters as Oliver St. John Gogarty and F. R. Higgins, and on the other by young writers — Austin Clarke and Patrick Kavanagh, among the poets — who were intent on modifying the agenda set by their elders. Those who differently looked to Joyce as an exemplary figure, and who were not content to work Joyce's early realistic vein, found little support. They mostly went abroad, and their recognition at home was delayed to the nineteen-sixties. I refer, of course, to Samuel Beckett, Denis Devlin and Brian Coffey — the generation which New Writers' Press did so much to recover and which also included Charles Donnelly, Niall Montgomery, George Reavey, Brian O'Nolan and the older figure of Thomas McGreevy.

The parallels between America, Britain and Ireland are not less instructive for being inexact. Irish writers of the thirties did not subscribe to a common cause, like the Objectivists. They were from a much more varied social background than Auden and his friends. Their interest in surrealism was generally more continuous, informed and detached than their English and American counterparts.

And just as the longer and more empiricist cultural tradition in England modified the reception of modernism, in contrast to its stronger development in America, so modernism in Ireland was modified by other factors. These include the fact that the beginnings of Irish modernism in the eighteen-nineties were not renewed in the next generation after 1910; the solitary pre-eminence of Yeats among poets; a more self-conscious and politically active nationalism; the peculiar role of the Abbey Theatre; the exile of Joyce; a smaller population; the different cultural and political relations with Britain, the Continent and America.

Samuel Hynes has demonstrated how the literature of the thirties in England developed according to the logic of a five-act drama[1], and the decade completes an era in a way which is not matched in America and Ireland. The central issues in American writing, which centred as in England on Marxism, did not reach crisis-point in the Spanish Civil War and did not work themselves out until after the fall of Senator McCarthy. The decade was similarly protracted in Ireland. The depressed socio-economic-political situation continued through the forties and even nineteen-fifties, and it intensified before the country slowly recovered. What elsewhere was experienced as a world war was known here as the Emergency. Post-war recovery did not take place, and cultural deprivation was acute to the extent that it was barely recognised.

In particular, unlike their American and English counterparts, Irish writers of the nineteen-thirties lived in a society where a political revolution on behalf of democracy and self-determination had actually happened within their lifetime. Irish modernism had begun in the eighteen-nineties, a generation earlier than in America and England, and the relation between art and life, which caused anguish to writers as different as Oppen and Stephen Spender, had already been confronted by Yeats. For the poets and dramatists of the Revival, Romantic Ireland was dead and gone some years before 1916.

The issues of the nineteen-thirties appeared for Irish writers in a rear-view mirror, separate and the other way round. Popular revolution had already proved itself to be bourgeois, and freedom as a nation imposed other, severely-felt constraints. Also, because of the different history of early and late modernism in Ireland, it contained a strong mimetic, anti-modernist element. The result was that Frank O'Connor and Sean O'Faolain shared the same dismissive attitude towards experiment as Yeats. The two of them dismissed *Work in Progress* in terms identical with Karl Radek's

---

1. *The Auden Generation: Literature and Politics in England in the 1930s* (London: The Bodley Head, 1976).

at the 1934 Soviet Writer's Congress, for its privatizing and specializing of reality and language[2].

The choice for writers like Beckett and Coffey was therefore not between Yeats and Marx but between Yeats and Joyce, not whether to join the Communist Party but whether or not to leave the country, not between art and life but between two different kinds of art, each of which contains implications about the way to live. The dilemma of the Irish writer seems at face value more literary and arcane than the choices insisted upon by Christopher Caldwell and Anthony Blunt in the pages of *Left Review*, or explored by Lionel Trilling in *The Middle of the Journey*, but it is not at all.

It is worth beginning with a rehearsal of these matters because Devlin has so often been taken as a representative of an "alternative tradition". He has been read as an international experimentalist born into a time when Ireland looked inwards, when he found no readers, and who waited to find recognition from a later generation, like Niedecker in America or Bunting in England. It seems to me, on the contrary, that Devlin was self-consciously and proudly an Irish poet, though self-consciousness and pride are checked by self-possession and restraint. Again, his reputation as a difficult and particularly "literary" poet has obscured the fact that the way he wrote makes sophisticated political commentary, if that is what readers are looking for.

Devlin chose not to write in the empiricist Irish tradition continued by Clarke and Kavanagh, and he shared interests and friendship with those who left Ireland like Coffey and Beckett. But he was from the beginning confident about the kind of writing he wanted to do, and his confidence did not falter though his writing changed. He did not suffer the rejection and sense of exclusion which Coffey records in *Missouri Sequence*. He did not stop writing or publishing, like Oppen, Bunting or McGreevy. In particular, it is helpful to recognise that he did not share the views on Irish writing in the thirties promulgated by Beckett and by Coffey, which are more widely known. At

2. For O'Faolain, see Robert H. Deming (ed), *James Joyce: The Critical Heritage* (London: Routledge and Kegan Paul, 1970) II 392, 397 esp; for O'Connor, ibid II 515-8; for Radek, ibid II 624-6.

best, he might be said to have shared in those views, which is a different matter. His own writing proceeds from a reserved position.

Thus, the most widely-advertised formulation of the position of the Irish writer in the thirties is Beckett's in the August 1934 issue of *The Bookman* under the pseudonym "Andrew Belis"[3]. He defines the position as a choice between Yeats, the Twilighters and their later representatives, on the one hand, and Joyce, Paris and self-conscious experiment on the other. Though the definition is unusually clear-sighted and retrospectively accurate, it is in advance of its time. It is an exacerbated analysis, which formulates a choice as a dilemma and thereby distorts it. It bears the same relation to reality as an infra-red photograph which obliterates contours. There is no evidence that other writers at the time felt the choice so acutely. Certainly Devlin, while he shared many of Beckett's views and occupies a crucial place in Beckett's formulation, was both more relaxed and more confident in the way he held these views.

Again, the views that Coffey expressed to Michael Smith and elsewhere[4] are an extrapolation from his earlier experience and should not retrospectively be imposed on it. At the earlier time, he had other interests and ambitions. For instance, he applied for a lectureship at University College Dublin, which would have enabled him to return, even as Devlin resigned a lectureship at UCD in order to leave. Whatever about Devlin's exemplary place in Coffey's later argument, the aims, scope and achievements of the two proceeded from separate assumptions.

Coffey developed his notion of an alternative tradition in Irish writing towards the end of the fifties and during the time he spent editing Devlin's poems. Devlin is central in Coffey's interpretation in a way in which Beckett is not, whatever Beckett's individual achievement. Devlin stands for a kind of poetry which sets the surrounding, better-known tradition in perspective. It

---

3. Collected in *Disjecta: Miscellaneous Writings and a Dramatic Fragment* ed Ruby Cohn (London: John Calder, 1983) 70-6.

4. Michael Smith "Irish Poetry Since Yeats: Notes Towards a Corrected History" *Denver Quarterly* V (Winter 1971) 1-26; Brian Coffey "A Note on Rat Island" *University Review* (Dublin) III: 8 (1966) 25-8; etc.

is dedicated to art before self-interest or self-expression. It is moved by contained confidence that does not have to seek for reassurance or curry favour. It contains values which might be said to be Irish, though they are unlikely to appeal to tour-operators or politicians.

What Coffey says and implies could be true. One would like it to be true because his vision of an Irish tradition is larger and more generous than what it argues against. It is nonetheless a vision, in the short term a polemic, and one involuntary consequence is that careless readers have confused what he says on his own behalf with what he says in his capacity as editor and glossator. His concern with the Revival as an episode in a longer tradition is prompted by different interests from Devlin's, his animus against the example of Yeats is stronger, his interest in experiment is more restless. It is important to disentangle his sense of history from Devlin's because it obscures differences and qualifications — for instance, Devlin's relation to Yeats and his relationship to English writing of the thirties.

II

Devlin's views on other writers and the literary tradition, his relation to them and his place in it, can be deduced from his reviews and articles in *Ireland Today, The Sewanee Review* and *New World Writing*, and can be supplemented by Coffey's memoir.[5] The reviews cover a wide range of authors — Irish, English, American and French. He is less enthusiastic about *symbolistes* like Baudelaire and Mallarmé than Coffey has been, and more enthusiastic and informed about Renaissance writers like Montaigne, Maurice Scève and Racine.

Despite his reputation as the most European among his generation of Irish writers, his acquaintance with Italian and Spanish poetry is slight compared to Beckett's, whereas his familiarity with English and American writers is more confident. He is less interested in the Pound-Williams tradition than Coffey

5. "Of Denis Devlin: Vestiges, Sentences, Presages" *University Review* (Dublin) II: 11 (1963) 3-18.

subsequently became, and much more in English writers of Auden's generation. Allen Tate and Robert Penn Warren became his sponsors soon after he arrived in America, and Warren wrote of the effect made on them when *Lough Derg* was submitted to *The Sewanee Review*.[6] It is a poem which might seem to have much in common with New Critical, Southern Agrarian values.

Among Devlin's unpublished poems, *Transition: To a Violent Communist*, written in Dublin in 1934, is addressed to someone like his college contemporary, Charles Donnelly, while *España España* is concerned with the bombing of Republican troops and the fall of Barcelona. Published poems like *News from the Eiffel Tower* and *Argument with Justice* are written with a particular awareness of issues under discussion in contemporary writing in England, as they appeared from outside English circles.

However, the pattern that can be discerned in Devlin's critical remarks is less interesting than his distinctive manner. He reads in a way which is entirely informed and entirely in control. His conclusions are continually evaluative. Even tentative judgements are made firmly. He has an exact place for everything, but the schema is withheld. The individuality of his position rests in a style, not in promulgating an interpretation. So he writes about Auden's *For the Time Being*, and about John Lehmann's *New Writing*, and Robert Lowell's first volume *Land of Unlikeness* and Laura Riding's *A Trojan Ending* and French Classicism. Each book is courteously received and placed, but in a way which declines to advertise a criterion apart from excellence.

When Devlin does offer a scheme, and interpretation, it is so non-controversial as to appear bland. In his introduction to a selection of ten contemporary Irish poets in 1953, he says merely that some tend to be more concerned with Irish subject-matter and more traditional in their style ("Celtic") and that others are more experimental and international ("metropolitan"). The introduction is emphatically not a fighting one, and the choice of poets and poems is even-handed. One might compare Michael Smith's quite different selection from poets of Devlin's own

6. "Denis Devlin: A Recollection" *Éire Ireland. Weekly Bulletin of the Department of External Affairs* (Dublin) No. 493 (5 September 1960) 6.

generation in *Lace Curtain* No. 4[7], and, even more important, its different kind of motivation.

The same lack of programmatic understanding is apparent in the authors who evidently meant most to Devlin: Hopkins, Racine, Goethe, Scève, Montaigne. He had dealings with revolutionary surrealists like Éluard and conservative Southerners like Tate. He translated a good deal of St.-John Perse sympathetically, he had wide contacts with literary circles in Rome in the years before he died, yet the circle of literary friendships does not constitute an agenda. They have been selected on Devlin's terms, for discernible private reasons, but his only apology for them is for their different kinds of pre-eminence. It is important that his most fluent and attractive piece of critical writing is an anecdotal memoir, concerned with the way the Perse translations were made.[8]

Devlin's enthusiasms are not of a kind which enter his writing in the way that Joyce or Dante enter into Beckett's, to be worked with or against. It is typical of Devlin that he never met Yeats or Joyce in person. He appears very early to have possessed a kind of self-confidence and sense of self-determination that did not need either to follow fashion or to surround itself with the sense of belonging to a school. He remains somewhat aloof from the writers he acknowledged. The allusions to Keats and Whitman (and Marvell?) at the opening and close of *The Death of Michael Collins* reinforce local meanings but these meanings do not depend on literary politics. They are not points of leverage, like the allusions to Yeats and Joyce in Coffey's *Death of Hektor*, where, as parallels are established, reputations are unsettled.

Devlin's sense of his place in Irish poetry has to be deduced, and the way he occupies that place is more important than its location. It evidently cannot be considered apart from the political and social matters he treats in his poetry. He was conscious of recent Irish history — the Rising, the founding of the state, the way that revolutionary feeling became bureaucratized, the compromises involved as ideals work themselves out in history.

---

7. Published in 1971 by New Writers' Press; reissued as *Irish Poetry: The Thirties Generation* (Dublin: Raven Arts Press, 1983).

8. "St.-John Perse in Washington" *Cahiers de la Pléiade* (Paris) X (1960) 86-9.

He was particularly conscious of Ireland in relation to Europe (France, England), and to America and Asia to a lesser extent: their different kinds of culture and the values these kinds embodied. In the broader view, after considering Ireland in relation to its then-recent past, he was less interested in Celts and Normans, or the Irish eighteenth-century, or the vagaries of nineteenth-century Irish nationalism than in values as they might be pictured in places — Paris and Munich, Annapolis and Angkor, even (around Dublin) the West Pier of Dun Laoghaire harbour, the Grand Canal, the station on the now-defunct DS&E line at Stillorgan.

His view is generalizing and sceptical with respect to particular occasions. As he said in his 1953 selection of Irish poets:

> The publicly successful periods for Irish poetry have occurred at moments of national unity in national revolutionary ferment; and this was particularly so in the early decades of the century when the literary and political movements interacted so fruitfully in the general impulse towards independence.[9]

His poem celebrating news of revolution, *Bacchanal*, exactly — and only — concerns such a moment of fruitful excitement. It is a nineteen-thirties poem in the English sense, and might be compared with poems by Spender and C. Day Lewis, but because revolution in Ireland had already taken place this is observed from a later, more considered position. The poem is thereby about more than political revolution. It is about those who work for revolution, from the outside, and it contains a dimension of pathos as well as hope which connects it with *Memo from a Millionaire*.

The poem *The Death of Michael Collins* can likewise be misunderstood as a naive party-political poem, as it has been by Seamus Deane.[10] But its subject is again focussed in a

---

9. *New World Writing* (New York) No. 4 (October 1953) 257.

10. "Irish Poetry and Nationalism: A Survey" *Two Decades of Irish Writing* ed Douglas Dunn (Manchester: Carcarnet, 1975) 11. Compare Brian Coffey's response in "Denis Devlin: Poet of Distance" *Place, Personality and the Irish Writer* ed Andrew Carpenter (Gerrards Cross: Colin Smythe, 1977) 140-1.

particular way on a general theme, and it needs to be read alongside *Mr. Allen*, which is neither less nor more political. All three poems are about moments of originating, inspiriting change, seen from different points of view.

The point of view of *Bacchanal* is in the expressive present, and complications are kept to the borders of the picture. *Michael Collins* is written from the point of view of age contemplating youth. *Mr. Allen* is written from the point of age contemplating youth, which in turn is contemplating another's age contemplating his own separate youth, and in which the "originating, inspiriting moment" is perhaps an invention. It deploys some of the same images as the "Irvine" section of *The Heavenly Foreigner* to a different effect.

What happens afterwards to the originating moment of revolution is explored in different ways in *Old Jacobin, Anteroom: Geneva* and *Memoirs of a Turcoman Diplomat*. The first was originally titled *Fugitive Statesman*, and in its unrevised form more obviously had to do wih an Irish Republican, perhaps someone like Eamon de Valera. *Geneva* is more sour and succinct. *Turcoman Diplomat* is the most complicated in the way it balances hope against not-caring, a time of promise against sad experience. The poems are differently ironic, sad and sceptical. They connect with contemporaneous writing in England on behalf of revolution, and make up a detached commentary on it. Sometimes, as in *Pays Conquis*, Devlin's commentary is even couched in Auden's language.

The kind of place Ireland is is made clear in the title-poem, *Lough Derg*. Its barrenness preserves one such originating moment clearly. As the "Galway" section of *The Heavenly Foreigner* puts it, "Strong as a fortress, shining as an early fortress." The material inability of Ireland to contribute to the process of European history, except through emigration, preserved it from compromises which are evident in richer, more central cultures. The relevance of this part of Ireland to the idea that Ireland has of itself is closer to McGreevy's view than that of W. B. Yeats.

Devlin states the same idea negatively, in satirical poems like *Encounter* and *Jansenist Journey*. *Annapolis* also appears to me to be about the same theme, though warmly as seen by an appreciative guest. The latest comers to the New World are marginalised by respectability; revolution has become cosy and familiar; American society has left behind what brought it to birth.

> But then, it is not Hans Andersen, the monuments
> Of power lour as in any London. Cadets conduct
> Camera-fans to the Governor's Residence
> To the Capitol and the Revolutionary General
> Leading ghosts on his enthusiastic stone horse.

The same values are celebrated positively in the ''Anatolia'' section of *Turcoman Diplomat* or even, oddly, in *The Passion of Christ*.

The Passion of Christ is composed on the premise celebrated in *Lough Derg*. The method is apothegmatic. Spaces open round episodes in the narrative, and to the extent that it is more fragmentary and spare, it becomes more resistant to explanation. The method runs counter to justification and theology, against accumulated ceremonial. It celebrates irrational, impractical acts of faith (''Veronica's Veil'').

The treatment of the two thieves bypasses theology and frames the problem of divine justice in terms of human understanding, as one of syntax. The words of the bad thief are merely jumbled and confused. In contrast to the Irishness celebrated by the Anglo-Irish (Protestant) Revival, the poem articulates a barer, sparer idea. The treatment of the two thieves might be contrasted with Beckett's in *En attendant Godot*, and, if the poem becomes an apology for what is Catholic and Irish, it is this in terms more diffuse than theological or political meanings.

The themes of Justice and God are linked in Devlin's poetry with his attitude towards women — that is, his love poetry is continuous with the themes I have been discussing. His attitude has been summarized by Brian Coffey in his introduction to the Dolmen edition of *The Heavenly Foreigner*; and what I want to stress here is that Devlin's love poems are continuous with his poems about society and religion, in showing how ideals enter time. The *Lough Derg* volume is arranged so as to make this point, moving as it does from poems concerned with justice to poems about love (beginning with *The Lancet*).

In the simplest biographical sense, all the love poems are about an early experience in Munich, celebrated in *Little Elegy* and referred to at the close of *The Colours of Love*.

> At the Bar du Départ drink farewell
> And say no word you'll be remembered by;
> Nor Prince nor President can ever tell
> Where love ends or when it does or why.
>
> Down the boulevard the lights come forth
> Like my rainflowers trembling all through the Spring,
> Blue and Yellow in the Celtic North . . .
> The stone's ripple weakens, ring by ring.
>
> Better no love than love, which, through loving
> Leads to no love. The ripples come to rest . . .
> Ah me! how all that young year I was moving
> To take her dissolution to my breast!

Yet the biographical occasion is too simple to explain away the continuance and enlargement of the theme, which is carried in the titles — *Farewell and Good, Renewal by her Element,* feeding forward continually as *Vestiges* and *Love from Time to Time*. Devlin's love poems employ the same celebratory terms of colour, warmth and movement as his poems about history and epistemology. They have the identical theme of *Welcome My World*.

This is why *Est Prodest* occupies such a significant position in each of Devlin's two complete collections, *Intercessions* as well as the *Lough Derg* volume. It is a poem which traces the breaking down of bonds of solitude, the waking to embrace others, the freeing of impulses. In *Est Prodest* lies the beginning of *The Heavenly Foreigner*: love of justice, love of God, love of women are aspects of the same love. Scève is as much an influence on his ideas of political revolution as on *The Colours of Love*. Devlin's view of love is the same as his view of Ireland: sceptical, historical, relativistic on the one hand; radically, idealistically, poetically simple on the other.

III

I have probably said enough about the interrelation of themes in Devlin's poems. The themes are manifested as a quality of style, which is ultimately more interesting. I say more interesting because the way the themes work themselves out shows them as they actually live. The poems open up areas in which the themes are brought to a provisional formal balance.

One of the most obvious features of Devlin's style is the way he manages transitions. The way his poems move forward contains an habitual life. Stasis is barren (*Royal Canal, Est Prodest, Obstacle Basilisk*), yet perfection does not survive change (*Boy Bathing*), except in imagination (*Mr. Allen*). Stillness is associated with cold, whiteness, silence and death; movement with colour, warmth, life and music. This pattern of imagery links the earliest-written poems with the latest, and is an instinctive dimension of their vocabulary. The belief that the moment which originates change is the most pure, and that life inheres in change and movement away from that beginning, is nevertheless a paradox. It follows that the kind of movement which distinguishes Devlin's poems is self-conscious, self-checking. The poems turn over in their length, take off suddenly in unanticipated directions, double back.

The moment of transition frequently hinges on a line-ending which can open either way. A word has a terminating meaning at the end of a line, then becomes a trap-door into a different meaning as you read onwards. Dillon Johnston's chapter on Devlin in *Irish Poetry after Joyce* comments on several examples of this feature in variant forms,[11] and it is related to the way Devlin uses rhyme. His stanza forms are characteristically simple, and what is important to him is the way rhyme can facilitate the kind of transition I have described.

The patterned, patterning element of stanza-forms is less often exploited than the ability of rhyme to impart a sense of movement. One might contrast Brian Coffey, whose

---

11. South Bend, Indiana: University of Notre Dame Press/Dublin: The Dolmen Press, 1985, Chapter 4 (169-74 esp). See also Brian Coffey "About the Poetry of Denis Devlin" *Poetry Ireland* (N.S. Dublin) No. 2 (Spring 1963) 76-86.

characteristic effects are achieved within lines and unrhymed paragraphs. Devlin's poems veer and tack, change direction like his own *Windtacker Windjamming*. They make up poetry of compressed metaphor — literally, bearing across --, as opposed to Coffey's method of analogy or placing. Rhymes apply a tourniquet to feeling until it turns inside out, whereas the characteristically steady, iambic pulse of Coffey's lines accumulates feeling more slowly, layer by layer, which then turns aslant.

Devlin's idiosyncratic titles are related to the same twisting, energized effect. They are frequently elliptical, and reverse their meaning under the pressure of being applied. Take, for example, *The Statue and the Perturbed Burghers*. The poem is about the arts of space and time, stillness and movement, sculpture and music. But the burghers, you come to realize, are not perturbed and that is what is cause of perturbation. It is the poet who is perturbed by the coincidence of art with burgherly values. At the same time, you come to see that the statue symbolizing "rare immersion in stillness" is ultimately less exciting to the poet than other symbols in which inhere other values: a living woman (not a sculptured boy), performance and music (not achieved sculpture), emblematized by crimson and privacy (not by pearly, public marble). A more accurate title would be *The Burgherly Statue and the Perturbed Poet*.[12]

Other titles which in different ways put a topspin onto meaning include *Summer Jujube, Daphne Stillorgan, Eve in my Legend*, and, slightly differently, *West Pier* and *Royal Canal*. Devlin's changes of title in manuscript are of interest for this very reason, that they register these changing perspectives. Other titles again are simpler, just as other poems proceed in a more directly continuous manner. Very often, the poems which proceed more straightforwardly and continuously are dramatic monologues. Then they are complicated by irony, or at least some kind of qualification. What they say is set at a remove, and made oblique by some qualification, imported by the supposed speaker. Besides *Bacchanal*, consider *D'Artagnan makes a Case* and *Memo*

---

12. *Compare the relation of art to morality with, for instance, Auden in Museé des Beaux Arts*; also the first two parts of Stevens's *Owl's Clover* sequence published in 1937 — "The Woman and the Statue" and "Mr. Burnshaw and the Statue".

from a Millionaire. The simple movement of the lines evokes a sophisticated interpretation, because their full meaning depends on meanings which run counter to the lines you read.

The poems which appear to move more simply — often in longer, unrhymed lines — are sometimes in numbered or named parts which play against each other. This is a method of construction which characterizes Devlin's poems after the *Lough Derg* volume. Examples are *The Colours of Love, The Passion of Christ, Memoirs of a Turcoman Diplomat* and, very obviously, *The Heavenly Foreigner*. The method is an aspect of an enlarged, looser kind of structuring. Even the *Lough Derg* volume has simplified some of the effects of *Intercessions* by inserting more punctuation, as an examination of the poems which were carried forward will reveal.[13] Commas and full stops indicate choices where alternate constructions were evenly balanced. They guide and channel meanings to run forward without inhibition.

The meanings of Devlin's later poems, which are controlled by juxtaposition of larger elements, are mobile in a different way from his earlier poems. The movement from line to line in the later poems is usually more direct, but then the relation between larger groupings of lines complicates them in another way. Ambiguities are less a matter of local effect and more of adjusting larger perspectives. This, however, is another theme: the relation between Devlin's modifying point of view and his developing technique. It seems to me he was entirely consistent during the thirty years of his writing life.

Some aspects of Devlin's technique have been regretted and been a cause for complaint. For example, his habit of picturing values in terms of place might appear to involve a certain crude shorthand. The picturing of national characteristics in *Encounter* might appear on first reading to be a cartoon rather than a sketch, a reductive simplification. However, the point of the poem is not simply to set English values against French, crude materialism against culture and civilization. The French also are included in the point of view, and their very comfortableness is in turn to

13. Coffey records that Devlin was influenced by the example of Mallarmé in the *Eventails* (''Of Denis Devlin'' see note 5 above). He discusses Devlin's punctuation in relation to the charge of obscurity in ''About the Poetry of Denis Devlin'' 77-81 (note 11 above).

be seen as a kind of complacency. The poem continues the argument of *Lough Derg,* which precedes it in the collection, and this is in turn developed in *The Statue and the Perturbed Burghers,* which comes after. It is Jansenist, in Devlin's terms, in its scepticism towards fixed forms of material satisfaction.

To take another example, *Liffey Bridge* at first looks like a tourist's view of the issues involved by someone who was not a tourist, but the fact is the poem does not pretend to be a simple lyric credo. It is more complicated in that it works through a set of attitudes which correspond to the persons and scene imaged, which are those of the poet only in an oblique sense. Devlin is to be identified with the poem as a whole, of which he is in control, not with its separate parts, and with the whole as a condition of volatile equilibrium.

When the method is not understood it looks like the product of disabling detachment, snobbery. Devlin's way of handling ordinary syntactic transitions might appear equally to be the product of impatience, but the estimate equally would be wrong. Sense is elided, meaning is syncopated, because it has to be. The evolution of the poems in manuscript and through revised typescripts shows it was a feature he worked hard to attain. It was not the product of impatience which balks at hindrance, nor of sloppiness which cannot be bothered to clarify, but of energy consistently applied to a purpose which takes manifold directions. When the effect succeeds, it is exhilarating in a way few poets can rival.

It would be idle to pretend that the sense in Devlin's earlier poems does not sometimes break down, but the inner sense rarely does, perhaps never. The distinction is important, because, of the two kinds of consistency, that of pictorial imagery is the less important. I have suggested in another essay, with reference to *Memoirs of a Turcoman Diplomat,* that the irony which qualifies the meaning in some of the later poems does not always answer questions the poems have raised.[14] A deeper acquaintance with the poems and the way they came into being now makes me feel that Devlin knew exactly what effect he wanted to produce. If the ideals of the Turcoman Diplomat are at the end somewhat tarnished, so be it.

---

14. In *Advent. Denis Devlin Special Issue* (Southampton) No. 6 (1976) 9-14.

If there is a criticism to be made, it might be slightly different. Devlin delights in breaking moulds — in the title *Freedom No Object*, the emphasis is on the word *Object* —, but even his admirers have to concede the shorter poems are sometimes not long enough to enable the movement which they celebrate to take place. There is a danger that they will end up as merely anecdotes (*From Government Buildings*) or riddles (*Tantalus*). He wisely left a good many imagistic shorter poems — *Moments* — in manuscript. They remain notations. Devlin needs space to work through his preoccupations, characteristically, though in his late poems the emotion is not on as tight a rein as in the early and middle ones.

I also have reservations about some of Devlin's work in translation, which are connected to this same theme. Besides the translations collected in the present volume, he left perhaps as many again unpublished. They date from all periods of his life — from his schooldays to his last years in Rome. They are from French into Irish and English into French, and from French and German and Italian into English, from a much greater variety of kinds of author than those he published. Also, the manuscripts and typescripts show that Devlin worked on translation in exactly the same way as on his own poetry. He returned to earlier drafts and versions looking to see what could be made of them afresh, in the spirit of one encountering work to be explored for what could be made of it. The evidence suggests a conscious commitment to the logic of *poesis* rather than to the biographical occasions which might have given rise to poems, and the commitment is at once passionate and impersonal.

Even so, translation is not as central in his work as in Coffey's, nor as interesting as in Beckett's. This is because, while his commitment to the work of others was no different in kind to his other writing, it was in practice often possessed of lesser intensity. The processes of revision show that, whereas with his own poems he frequently overwrote their first occasion entirely, his sense of obligation as a translator made him work in a different and more circumspect way. It is clear that he sometimes turned to translation for relaxation or to meet a promise, not in order to explore issues continuous with and under the same pressure as his other verse.

In particular, though his Perse translations are never less than interesting, and though they consistently achieve a standard which has been rated superior to Perse's other translators, their relation to his central achievement needs to be objectively assessed. St.-John Perse's long lines and prose-poetry have a different, less urgent pulse than Devlin's own poems like *Bacchanal* and *Victory of Samothrace*. Nor is Devlin's translation as Coffey's might have been, in the profoundest sense critical. The business of translating Perse might also have contributed to the loosening of structure and local texture in Devlin's later poems which I have already noted.

IV

What do these observations amount to? What kind of poet is Devlin, and what is his place in twentieth-century and Irish poetry?

First, it helps to separate his career from some of the uses to which it has been put. His reputation in Ireland as an experimental and difficult writer is for the large part an accident. The diplomatic career which took him abroad made it too easy to dismiss or champion him as an "international" writer. In fact, he was clearly not a member of the avant-garde, whose starting point is polemic and whose career is defined in terms of opposition to the established canon. He did not write in the fashion of his time, in Ireland, but he did not write against it in the sense that, for instance, Charles Olson and Robert Duncan wrote against the American literary establishment. His concerns are neither combative nor revisionist. They are simpler and broader. In John Montague's words, "he wanted to write a poetry that would be as good as the best anywhere in the world.[15]

For Devlin, even to think in terms of a national literary tradition is provincial and limiting. His aim was like that of Joyce in fiction,

15. "The Impact of International Modern Poetry on Irish Writing" *Irish Poets in English* ed Seán Lucy (Cork: Mercier Press, 1973) 157.

to take the world as his province. Devlin looked to the writers from whom he took his bearings in the same way as Joyce looked to Hauptmann and Ibsen, Flaubert and Vico. They are writers against whom a writer measures his position — not from whom he borrows or hides behind. The result is, in Devlin's as in Joyce's case, a kind of writing which is less against its time than outside it. It is not a programmatic deviation from other writing of the nineteen-thirties but instead proceeds on a different, classic premise.

Other writers besides Devlin followed Joyce's rejection of the narrowly provincial ambitions of the Irish Literary Revival, and most of them, including Joyce, have had problems of audience. It would seem as if, when a writer looks beyond an unsympathetic local audience to another one — perhaps no larger, but more widely spread --, he courts the risk of writing with no audience at all. Joyce in the end found an audience for *Ulysses*, though it took several decades to become an educated one, and the audience for *Finnegans Wake* is still being created. Beckett discovered an audience through the accidental success of *En attendant Godot*, after decades of obscurity ("Seventeen copies sold, of which eleven at trade price to free circulating libraries beyond the seas. Getting known."); but he came almost at once to feel that his celebrity rested on misunderstanding.

Joyce and Beckett looked beyond the confines of Ireland to define their purposes, and, by design and accident, they found their best readers in mixed, international circles whose perceptions were then re-imported. The process conforms to Stephen Dedalus's observation "that the shortest way to Tara was *via* Holyhead." Devlin, however, has not found a sufficient body of readers abroad or at home. His writing is available to anyone who will master its language, its procedures, on its own terms. It has, as I have tried to show, a good deal to offer anyone who is prepared to learn how to read it. It has found receptive readers and strong advocates, but they have been few and widespread.

Ethnomusicologists assume that the identity of music depends on more than what is written down; that it depends on a background of attending to it, absorbing it, learning it, repeating it.[16] The ability to read a score is not the same as being able to hear the music. In the same way, Devlin's poetry reminds one that poetry is more than the words on the page, that poetry comes into existence as a part of a repertory. Patrick Kavanagh wrote in opposition to the Revival during the nineteen-thirties, but his method was to set parish above province, and from the beginning he could count on a small but sufficient body of readers who could hear him. Devlin has not been able to count on a proper hearing, despite the respect he has been accorded at large.

One might compare other writers who, in our time, have in different ways stood apart and argued for a more ample understanding of poetry: Laura Riding, Hugh MacDiarmid, Christopher Middleton, for instance. What such writers share and what sets Devlin at a distance from them is the way they have been marked by their isolation. They have all in some way been maimed by their failure to win recognition. Devlin was not, because, from the beginning, his poetry engaged the world differently, on terms which had simultaneously more to do with private need and utterly impersonal ambitions. In his Turkish diplomat's words, writing was to "Compose the absolute kingdom far in the sky." A better comparison would be with such other exiled inhabitants of imagined realms — "a placeless heaven rather than a heavenly place" — as, today, Miroslav Holub and Joseph Brodsky.[17]

Devlin did enjoy an international audience during the years he was in Washington. He gave poetry readings and published in a flurry of little magazines. Allen Tate and Robert Penn Warren described him, in 1963, as "one of the pioneers of the international poetic English which now prevails on both sides of the Atlantic" because they read *Lough Derg* in terms of Stevens' *Sunday Morning*, Eliot's *Gerontion* and Crane's *The Broken Tower*.[18] They gave him encouragement at a vital time by

---

16. Joseph Kerman "A Few Canonic Variations" *Canons* ed Robert von Halberg (Chicago: University of Chicago Press, 1984) 177-95.

17. The phrase is Seamus Heaney's in "The Placeless Heaven" *The Government of the Tongue* (London: Faber and Faber, 1988) 4. Heaney's argument is comparable to Devlin's, but differs as their poetry differs.

18. Introduction to *Selected Poems* (New York: Holt, Rinehart and Winston, 1963) 13, 14. It might be remarked that, while Devlin's reading in Eliot is known and obvious, his early manuscripts contain verses addressed to Hart Crane.

introducing him to other writers, recommending him to editors, arranging for reviews. To the extent that Devlin had more readers than Beckett or Coffey throughout the nineteen-forties, he was probably valued for what Tate and Warren found in him.

Even so, the reputation he enjoyed rested partly upon misunderstanding. Whatever his poems appear to share with Anglo-American modernism is given a different cast and direction by the different premises on which they rest. It is not surprising that Randall Jarrell — perceptive and particular critic that he was — savaged Devlin's collection from the wartime years, making clear that it required a reading different from the one he was prepared to give it.[19] He attacked it for its method of proceeding from instant to instant concentrated upon the parts, for its consciousness of surface, for its allusiveness, for the very things that distinguished *Lough Derg* from other volumes of which he approved.

I explained earlier how Devlin never experienced the disillusion that befell his generation in England and America. His detachment was not withdrawal or the result of alienation: it had always been part of his sense of public commitment. Consequently, though the features of style in which it found expression — irony and indirection, complexity and inconsecutiveness — might have appeared familiar to New Critical readers, they came from another background. In the end, as Jarrell was able to perceive, his poetry has a different, declarative pulse. Notice the number of titles and first lines which begin with a definite article followed by the subject. Notice the way that lines which push beyond rhyme extend into rhythmical prose. The proof of any poem is in its rhythm — what Theodore Roethke called "the chief clue to the energy of the psyche" --, and the effects condemned by Jarrell are positive, not counterfeit.

Such poetry seeks to be classic in seeking to establish itself in relation to the best that has been written, wherever and at whatever time. It is impersonal, in that it abjures the sense of

19. "The Poet and his Public" *Partisan Review* (New York) XIII:4 (September - October 1946) 488-500 (492-3 esp). Jarrell toned down his criticism in the collected version, "Poets" *Poetry and the Age* (New York: Knopf, 1953) 220-36 (224-6 esp). It is answered in detail by Brian Coffey, in the essay referred to in note 10 above.

a lyric I. "I would like a discourse from which the middle terms have been dropped," Devlin told Brian Coffey, and Coffey remarks, "He worked at the level of things deindividualised without having become abstractions."[20] It is also purposeful, in a way that distinguishes it from surrealists from whom he learnt, like Breton and Éluard. Thus his lyrics proceed from a way of seeing which is ideal, and the ideal is what is shared. Put another way, his writing explores a world shorn of accident, even if the world is summoned into being for manifestly personal reasons.

Beckett quoted and praised *Est Prodest* in 1934, when it was still in process of being written, and I have remarked on the centrality of the poem in Devlin's writing. Beckett responded to the same dualistic theme in a different way, which is a reminder of another starting-point the two writers share and from which they diverge. For Beckett, the acutely problematic relation between self and non-self was cause for despair. For Devlin, it was a relation to be worked through. I have suggested *The Passion of Christ* might be read against *En attendant Godot*. All of Devlin's writing might be read as an affirmative response to a dilemma he shared with Beckett — in its literary, moral and theological aspects.

Of *Intercessions*, Thomas McGreevy remarked, "He has something of the riotous poetry-making quality of Francis. He sees poetry everywhere and identifies himself poetically with all the phenomena about him. . . . And whatever the obstacles, he believes in the ultimate realization of perfect existence."[21] The radiant light which plays about these poems is somewhat qualified in Devlin's subsequent collection and after, in the sense that it is seen in more complicated ways, but it is in no way denied. The starting-point, from which Beckett drove himself into a cul-de-sac, and upon which he afterwards built an art of shrinking contradiction, set the terms for Devlin's writing to expand, loosen, grow.

Devlin's poems are constructs in which an idea is worked through. They have a necessity born of the purpose of making, because there is no other way to achieve the kind of resolution

---

20. "Of Denis Devlin: Vestiges, etc." 17, 12.

21. "New Dublin Poetry" *Ireland Today* (Dublin) II:10 (October 1937) 82.

sought. *Est Prodest* is paradigmatic in this respect. It registers the progress from stifled inarticulacy to the free flow of expression. Its terms appear abstract, but they condense, in Beckett's phrase, according to "inverted spiral of need."[22] The subject is entirely contained in the writing, because it can only be worked out through the writing. Its conclusion is positive and, though its terms appear general, they have connections with Devlin's views on other subjects.

As Beckett went on to say in the same essay, which he wrote in response to the *Times Literary Supplement* review of *Intercessions:*

> It is naturally in the image that this profound and abstruse self-consciousness first emerges with the least loss of integrity. To cavil at Mr Devlin's form as overimaged (the obvious polite cavil) is to cavil at the probity with which the creative act has carried itself out, a probity in this case depending on a minimum of rational interference, and indeed to suggest that the creative act should burke its own conditions for the sake of clarity.

This is not to be read as a simple defence of disconnected images and surrealist obscurity, as it has been. Beckett is describing a kind of poetry where images and the relation between images constitute the life of the poem. Constitute is not the right word, because it obscures the mobility of the transactions which take place, and the provisional nature of the conclusions reached.

Such a use of poetry places it in a central position, so that one can understand Devlin's almost hallowed sense of poetic vocation. The extraordinarily full collection of manuscripts he left behind, written on every kind of scrap, on every conceivable occasion, preserved and reworked at widely separated intervals, shows a mind immersed in poetry in order to live. Poetry is need, interrogation, at a level where theories and prejudices have to be put aside. Its purpose is described by the title, *Intercessions*. It is "rhetorical question less the rhetoric," to quote Beckett yet

---

22. *Intercessions by Denis Devlin*, first published in *transition* (Paris) No. 27 (April-May 1938); *Disjecta* 91-4. The quotation in the next paragraph is from the same source.

again. It eschews faction, though it need not avoid treating factious issues. It has nothing to do with gossip, though it can contain fun. It is wholly in earnest, though it sometimes works through to conclusions with a ballast of irony. It differs from Coffey's sense of making in its different sense of rhyme and rhythmic grasp. It differs very obviously from Beckett's in its consistent, though not always unclouded optimism. The aims of the three writers are identical, even if there are more than these three ways to achieve their aim.

The obstacles to understanding poetry of the kind Devlin wrote are sometimes held to be references which can be footnoted, which is nonsense. Such obstacles are imaginary, and less important than the divide which any reader must cross to begin to follow the creation of individual poems. How the divide is to be crossed I do not know; nor do I know why readers — "gentle skimmers" — should make the effort to cross it, unless they are persuaded by the recommendations of readers like McGreevy, Beckett and Coffey. This introduction has said nothing more than they have previously said, although at much greater length.

INTERCESSIONS
(1937)

The Alembic

Heart, beneath monotonous accident
This stillblowing wind springs
No rain no rain enmeshing
Multiple infant feet of aspirant winds:
Least hindrance possible against
Cloistral lashes shut on folded cheeks
Sanction also with a poisoned blessing
Vital examen, for your mining teeth.

Blood's aromatic in my breath, a respite
The wind may unwax my summer, let the
Accountant suspend work, wipe his misty glasses
The wind pads almost noiseless like a cat
Do not reject its suave caresses, Heart.

Death and Her Beasts, Ignoble Beasts

The dried pus of vultures drags the horizon
The noble beasts retired, their turn now, dried
Mouths of my fears are death's vultures craving saliva:
They would feed sick life on the smashed mouths of the
  weak
Whose nostrils death has plugged with stale love-smells
And suicide charms with racked face in a wall of marble,
Their eyes decharged have numbness that looks like peace.

Smeller-out of strangers! curious Death
Your noble beasts were not fearful for they
The emerald bergs of doom, Cybele and the drums,
Startled my stupor into spite at least:
Now your corrupt sweet pleading through my friends
Smoothes me like cambric on an infant's flesh
You would enchant with physical dances me
That cannot afford to believe your vultures peacocks.

Unexplained tears suddenly blur my courage
And desert movements in the breast shaking
The forts I built so well already ravaged
By sleep by the cold by the intransigent light
Make your back-alleys seem imperative
There is none so much as you, none you, I think of.

But I turn to move. The antarctic world-specked dream
Grows without sound like flowers, man's bit of air
Throngs deafening ears that could distinguish once
Noises of rivers among the noises of seas:
Yet, Sacker of crumbling towns, I will not agree
To the proposal of peace you made to my friends.

Attack me in the dark, I'll extreme fear
With the first of all landscapes given its eyes
In the frantic group of naked man and horse;
With the cheering of shredded men in lost forts
And to go on with, the length of to-day and to-morrow,
The evidence that lifting needles make the cloth.

Victory of Samothrace

Hammers musical round my head, hammers throbbing on
the roofs
Wary silence of brutal propellers that have suddenly burst
their speed.
All aboard all stations calling all in all in!
Smell in the rain of mown hay and thistles, old
Red of poppies, creeping warmth of remembered desire
Heads are markets for anarchic holdings
Are there no shoulders to lean on?
A sweet lady! not alas! the invented lady of stasis

The fingers of a black-gloved hand are tender and vicious on
my throat
I am snatched up and hurled into the air
Sweet lady! on this grey sea you are not preceded by
singing Dolphins, as was Aphrodite
But by discord of winds
Nor by the noise of drums, drums throbbing continuous
hammers
But are yourself the creator of tornado with your clothes
whirring about your knees like grouse rising
And your wings
Disturbing the exact harmony of the stars

Victory, winged Victory!

The sea is empty of fish beneath me and there are no ships
Otherwise I should cry for help
But making the best of my own bargain
I offer you as gages of faith
The beginnings all over again

The never to be forgotten, and
The supposed brightness of lamps in daytime

Winged Victory of Samothrace!

Let me be always in this state of grace
Keep me going on bribes like this, the unfinished
  handiwork of sunset
Be to me also for a sign
Of burgled outhouses round an inviolable family stone
As a priest uncertain among his mysteries when a bending
  candle-flame provokes forbidden images

A man is swung between two lilies tall as pines. Terror!
Increasing loudness of a thousand feet of men tramping
  down wooden stairs. Throbbing wooden stairs
I will make another prayer
Give me an object of art, a statuette of Diana: I will caress
  her limbs closely with my fingers

For these graces, spirit of movement, I will build you an
  altar, to be destroyed immediately,
And make offering of promise
Of heroes once again
Of women's eyes before love has drowned their sweetness.
The moment is poised in fear

Our Lady of Victory!

And your voice, which has the opulent contentment of a
  June stream, babbles
And I feel with relief:
Better in danger with a goddess than float safe like a barge
  on the sea:

Fingers again at my throat

Baptism by immersion in the numerous sea

As the water closes over me, I look up while life keeps interest
To see the impersonal gleam in your eyes
And the soft ebb and flow of your breasts.

THE STATUE AND THE PERTURBED BURGHERS

Emptied and pearly skulls
Lie humbly among the roots of the grass
The inhabitants know it only too well
Walking delicately
Under the trees
They have stayed this fluttering boy in tight marble
For a fresh similitude
Of their rare immersion in stillness
Planted foaming trees
For coolness

People of worth and wealth
Glancing with care at their modes of life
Walls cradles windows amber orchards

My watch ticks as loud as a sledgehammer in an empty
  street
Muffle the panting hours my fountain, disdain them
Boy with the beaked chin

The tendrils of fountain water thread that silk music
From the hollow of scented shutters
Crimson and blind
Crimson and blind
As though it were my sister
Fireflies on the rosewood
Spinet playing
With barely escaping voice
With arched fastidious wrists to be so gentle.

WINDTACKER WINDJAMMING

I really don't know what to think
As the wise cat said to the king
When big with proverb
But if it's proper
To get my bearings
At least I'm aware of
My sky changing its costumes all day long.

Sometimes a close-eyed steamer outside port
Keeping my eyes about me in these foreign parts
I refuse to budge
Till the pilot takes the bridge
Then in the warm arms of breakwaters pressed
Allow my hold to be cleared without protest:
Which housewife inability
To give without being guaranteed stability
Me more amuses
Unfortunately, than it distresses.

Sometimes a cloudburst of starlings
I take with exaggerated bombardment
Of silly chatter trees in Spring
Overwhelming groping speech that needed training.

Rarely when, a clever taxi
With discreet axles
I tow the line without jamming,
My thoughts get such a shock
They set up a most undignified screaming
Like a lot of schoolboy factory horns at one o'clock.

Usually a seaport on the west coast
On my last legs above the rodent sea standing
I doze most of the day to make the most
Of the night with sailors and gin and dance-tunes and
  candles
Because I know I'm going to totter
Into the sea some day;

And it will be so much the better
If I can slip off gaudily while on the batter
And without annoying the neighbours by piteous bawling
Let's hope I resign from myself gracefully
With no ill-feeling.

Liffey Bridge

Parade parade
The evening puts on
Her breath-stained jewels
Her shadowy past.

Trailing behind
Tired poses
How they all
Fulfill their station!
The young with masks and
The old with faces
Such an assassin
Such a world!

From the bridge they admire
Their foolish reflection
Drowning in birth,
Man's face and centuries
In rivers with stars
Fugitive wheatfields
Giving no harvest . . .
Here's poulticed peace.
If dreaming of death
Unheavened could but rend them
With anger or envy!

The pigeons creak
On rusty hinges
Turn to the window
Bright with oranges
And girls the girls

The gashed fruit
Of their mouths and smiles
Cute as the rims
Of their cock-eyed hats:

In limp doorways
They try out their heaven
They grind at love
With gritted kisses
Then eyes re-opened
Behold slack flesh
Such an assassin
Such a world!

Same with all the
Young and hopeful
Any relief will
Do for a spell
Then timid masks
Live into faces
Then there is quiet
Desperation.

The houses lean
Against the wind
Won't you give over?
Say, what about
That second coming?

Deaf quay walls.
Water wears
The stone away
And out on the river
The arc-lamp rays and the

Wind weave
Try to weave
Something or other
From flight and water.

GRADUAL

Why, how often, with first the matchlight knocking
  With little alluring jabs, drabness
    Of moist blankets,
Conceding laziness not even got from
  Pleasant defeat in dough splattered
    From arclamps;

In a flamingo of oil-geysers afire once for likeness
  I offered fire to the sun's fire at evening
    On roads westward;
Not even then convinced against exciting
  Metamorphosis, pheasants into beating
    Horses love-abreast;

Last, inevitable executioner, scythes handling
  For every prosperous disorder
    Foresight heartening,
Lighthouse, O regent of the seas trampling
  Jetsam, heady storms absorbing;
    Raper of darkness,

You struck, you tore the cry of the woman that loves most
  Thrown in the straw, warm beast-breath cylinders,
    No farmhands even . . .
Why, when elect, not fire the retaining bordels?
  Trifler of grace, from surrender shrinking,
    And frenzy of streets.

Daphne Stillorgan

The stationmaster is garrulous in
The modest station set in the glen
Bushes wink with brown birdwings
The benches spread their knees, present
Drowsy laps to the sun.
A white cat, scared, dangerous within
Egyptian memories considers
Like a marksman a celluloid ball on a water-jet
A tigermoth's fatal rise and fall
On her rank breath.

One shadow makes the whole sky shake
But I flick with instantaneous eyes
The next quick change before the change begins.
The water spouts are dried
The laurel leaves
Fixated in this colloidal summer.

The clean metronome of horses' feet on the road
Made anguish with clocks and rules which now
Silence beyond measure floods again
Though the trees' green bazaar and patches
Of light like muslin girls in forest lost.
And lost but after noisy pebble wrinkling
This scene became a pool in air limpid
Restoring to the inimitable Images
Reflections paled but smooth as smooth as smooth

Fuchsias revive and breathe through scarlet mouths
Rumours on wind:
Far-off the humid pounding of a train

Wind-cylinders boom along
Steel wires, the rails drone
Far-off thudding, trampling, thud
Of thousand pink-soled apes, no humorous family god
Southward a storm
Smashes the flimsy sky.

Vines virgins guard your red wine
Cross branching arms frail on breasts
Small showers will fall before the rain crowds
Use them to cool your rind-stiffening flesh
Writhing with blood for sap
To suck the insect-pointed air, the first threat
Of eager ravishers.

Scared faces lifted up,
Is the menace bestial or a brusque pleiad
Of gods of fire vagabond?
Quick, just in time, quick, just in time, ah!
Trees in light dryad dresses.

Birds (O unreal whitewashed station!)
Compose no more that invisible architecture.

In the Last Resort

Me seeing the seen, the prestige of death drives faint,
Coupled asynchronous like time and knowledge.
Lunar scaffolding, a decrepit star falls
Rotting eyelashes fall through fetid wind:
My eyes' tarnished jewels and bright jewels:
Lunar scaffolding bathed in equal light
New starlight reaches earth in safety.

Played as between each other they are grave
Not to be explained by winking of an eyelid
But as against death's cuff on my interrupting
Eyes where the bony earth and iron seas
Knuckle into passion brief and only, then
They are treasure and my affair. And the glittering style
That's named to death because he takes unrest
Comes simply from his being a jewel-thief.

BACCHANAL

Forerunners with knees flashing like scissors raced by the
  hostile telegraph wires,
Start for the ships with the news, Cut Through, all is
  against them despair inspires:
The poor made limp by want and cackling brainstopped
  youth, a seaweed crowd . . .
How the road that smokes through the mountains, whose
  pantherbounding shadows applaud, is loud
With the confident feet of pursuing criers, their eyes
  diamond with thousands of years
Of domination and lands held of fictitious papers by right
  of fears
Easy on which to maintain the sneering feet of the lovely
  lords of might,
They and the courtiers of prudence insured against danger
  of life and number and light.

Forerunners run naked as sharks through water, nose to
  their prey, have message by heart
Their thighs will be tackled, Look Out They're Away
  clipping the wind, they've gained on their start

The wind thrusts knives in their teeth, harrows the stubble
  of parched throats
The front line licks its fire, leaderless, can they cut their way
  to the boats?
They have never eaten nor drunk nor slept their fill, and
  have no quick-wit means,
Only envy learnt in feeding the shutfist pistoned right
  machines.
Canaille, canaille, what red horizons of anger for humbled

lives lie
Tumbled up in the old times, the long-fermenting now, canaille!
Tradition if wanted, you can taunt with bequeathed pain, unslaked hate,
For neither the slow-travelling signal from the pyramid builders comes too late,
In spite of imposed ignorance, No, nor intelligence from a brave new State.
Death, starvation among the corn and coal stored in bankrupt winter
Bent-rail backs of daily slaves and soiled skin under accosting banter
Of flashbabies in back-quarters: Where meetings froth loud to a rebel note.
Useless. For after smokescreen luxury penitent cocky plebeians trot
And putrescent tenements breed their vermin, tearing holes in occasional rags,
Fume from sour mouths of windows, whimper on senile quicksand legs.
Raucous the air and barb-tongued seasoned with tunes from slit-eyed bars,
Where living on credit in blabbing pints the anger of cities boozy stares
G.P.I. poxed brows Oh what the hell Plenty duties and damn all rights
They can't get away with it They shall pay for it Up to the neck in it Blast the Skites!

How shall we suffer the little children to come unto us, how shall we pay
For the ranged amorphous faces grey as the creased skies this guttering day?

While the pushbelly hunger-currency bankers cultivating the delicate flowers
Of their happy entrails, hand in hand dance around earth-produce pyres
And religious scarecrows navigate with downcast eyes this vale of tears?

Already immense shoulders heave edgeways through heavy bales of sleep
Force of confederate free flangewheels, O runners through breakage!
Give them the slip:
Those with hands like shrinking linen that deprecate the state of affairs,
Parsing their attitudes, fleas in intricate corridors of interlocking hairs,
Those that are Not so sure that the poor in pogrom will not be rather a Bore,
Lips bitter-sweet, they know by Culture they know Human Nature can grow no more;
Those that are Game to Grin and Bear it, those that the Wear and Tear Of, that hesitate,
Wagging advice faded and steaming as old maids' clothes before the grate,
Those that My Country, that Let Us Pray, that Drop by the Way, those that are Late . . .
Oh when damned by the sentence of guns advancing like ants in tragic line
And stowed away in Death, their own hungry mirror, it will be fine!

The blood beats drums in the runners' temples, the news is safe as a yacht in a cove
And hearts, throbbing squadrons of nocturnal seaplanes,

moving stars above
Stars fixed in the sea, it will be fine, the ground is cleared,
material stored,
With fervid violence Come forerunners release the news at
this anxious port.
Red trains lap up the licking rails, east the horizon snarls
alarms
Relief from the wheatfields, printing presses toss their
tresses with steel arms
Come up! Up up! The thunder at one with your voices in
order chants things
Are with you, rolling her rump Earth in bacchantic rumbas
grave swings,
Multiple antennae of blind gunnery tremble, invest the
fibrous night
And the armies' crystal shock makes laughter of girls in a
forest pool out of sight.

Is it true is it true, have you seen the syllables travel over
lips, have you seen
Beermugs whirled through battered lyrics, children ring
embrace on the green?
Bright women thrown in laughter, oh gay, oh nothing need
anything refuse,
Goldstocking legs in their white foam swinging, a country
singing joy of the news?

Joy Joy an unbetweened chorus crowds the air with sound
Burgeoning they feel surging more loud the birth of well-
being all around
While curveting aeroplanes, leaflets released, toss through
the matador swords of the sun
And the ships cheered by the seminal hail of the captain, by
the people won,

Draw white clothes on, make sure of the sea, open tanned
  arms with love and take
To the long white heather of the waves, a wind of towns in
  cry in wake.

Forerunners with eyes of dangerous landscapes silent among
  the cheering sigh
At the flocks of aeroplanes grazing at stall across the Spring
  prairies of the sky.

Communication from the Eiffel Tower

In the court darkness breathes heavily like a woman in
labour
Starlight hammers at wary roofs always at bay
Always at bay the houses carry their boatloads of sleepers
Through celestial channels of darkness upset with nightmare
Shying at the shallows of that feeble light, moon, that ally
of day.

What waitingroom dreariness fades on the bright rose
wallpaper!
Lamplight drips reluctantly over the windowsill
The air scaly with fish, disgust frictions my skin
Apprehension becomes china eyes become
A wavering plainchant trappist digging his gravesods
One sod per diem, and he stiffens as the vivid sweat
Stings in the roots of his hair.
Shame among the roots of life.
So far for me, turn round
I would roll in the plasmic multiplication of her hands'
Convulsive foam on waves which are
Crumbled by cliffs and their reiteration
Stifled at each birth, sucked back
Into the slack marine mass; and she
Fighting for me with any stimulant
Whispers GOBETHAU gesticulates GOBETHAU

That is ill-chosen I have called his bluff
Once from a balcony set at eagle height
He showed me air that first poured brown like glue
And then clotted rigid with human nerves
A saw tore at my forehead

Woman slapped up of ooze, not were you a red angel
  would
The dreaming whips of your arms into earth absorb me
A close unfabulous animal
Still less his laws you repeat, for as you love me
You take the approximate and safe; but speak ahead
''Whereas'' she states ''fortune and misfortune construct
  existence
For the fairer sifting of history
To the more fortune of our children's children
And whereas it is expedient to have heaven, of dark locality
  doubtless,
Made of distracted eyes the beacon while the hands bought
  off
In major labour nurse the treasury
Of the minority most virtuous
So, for that this misery of the many is necessary
Avert your countenance while my tribal groups of combat
In a terse putsch strike elsewhere for your sake
Besides our misery's mental, take this girl''
Well no, I must say
And your play of the fatal spy is good at that

GOBINEAU has enpimped you, you have all gone dame
With feathers and cooing curves as if I had made you
Keep off poisoner of seed pretty flint-flanks
Pivot of a fan of showgirls with a slow lilt to their hips
Will I come? But it is absurd, a bookworm, now, Will I
  mind my business?
Yes I know let me alone your only words are insane.

Let's have breakfast now to pretend it's morning
No, the bell corrodes the silence cover my mouth
Gentle when I am sleeping breathe girl O summer twilight

The fireflies of your gentle thoughts through my gnarled
thorntree nerves
Smile through my eyelids soothing as a shaded lamp

Let her not take thee with her eyelids
Let her not bemuse thee with her tongue
All the legends of love are unavailing
All the hawthorn of breasts is comfortless
All the periods of eloquence cannot smother
The monosyllables of these unwilling unbelievers
Scuffling for a foothold
Prayer choked in their throats
By puffs of irondust of their subsiding works
The prefects of society stare with taut eyes
Try not to hear the exact drumtaps at their ears
The imagined representation of distant barbaric invasions
A snap as of jaws breaking, the windbiffed empire buildings
Crack snap apart, become felled pines
Hesitating into their preying shadows
All the bearers of further tidings dry up such as docked
ships
All the squadrons of bladed flight
Humiliated, are black beetles so crass in bulk they
Cannot be said to creep but lurch.

GOBINEAU it is why will you keep on saying GOBETHAU?
How can you help, you cannot get the words right
Leave me, I'll not be sucked away from memory
Through any fistular brutish throat, how sweet
Brutal and sweet the mouth

GOBINEAU self-consuming plane
Pure, bitter and sombre as all
Defenders of the past in the obstinate ditches of sleep

Banking on the privileges of age
Which I tell you are no longer honoured
Why mock as weakling the hope of the weak for serene
years
Since you'll not be there, why mock, this dog in the
Manger, mangy mastiff, was not once of your masterful
kindness!
Preside so at this conference of the ancestors
It should be a courtmartial, they have betrayed
It should be courmartial with death, howso the urbane
Death at bay make smile our eyes with its grace
Because from the wretched their blood avariciously drips
And unheard stealthy as on wool
Famished hordes advance like silent skies.
The lidded anger of the oppressed
Stutters through chinks; and may it detonate!

The seas with lowered heads charge at breakwaters
Wildlife scythes my forest with scythes
And while the baying of rhapsodic women
March of the maenads bearing torches
Rises through the dissolute fens of my mouth
Gaping in front of surprising hands that drape
With fresh rain and light my turf and my dried bedrock
I hear the humming of my tower
Mounted on guard among the clouds

My tower is far and I have seen it seldom
I know that it is bound in the steel necessity
Of its own girders Time to one end willing
Time which is patience of man and hope of birth.

Unhappiness is easy shed
When any act can be fitted, even at command

As of simple recruits from their knees rising.
GOBINEAU in whom the egoist angels
Again iced our hearts and forced our hand
Into rebellion, beautiful
Disjointed mannequin, pomp is laughter
Just like any Caesar cracked
And you woman of dearth his procuress
Under the pierlamps cold wind and leavetaking and sad
  eyes
Other side of the gangway always
Cherished nostalgia gone, I am supplied
For needed nourishment with bread and wine
Worldaday my world my life my world

My blood sounds like a scream in the distance
Who then has drugged me?
Moths drag in the walls around my bed
A tall stinking lily turning to fungus
Splits; and the half-stems incline each side
The rotted voluptuousness of half-heads
GOBINEAU you would close me
In a circle of no thoroughfare
I am a bullfighter in this crossroads making passes for life
Among the slipping spears of the arclamps
While the eyes lined up on far benches drifted
Are yellow inhuman wounds

No movements no help alas not any help.
Their suffering looks faked and is not so,
And mine to them, but wrong, we know its cause.
What difficulty in landslides of marble
Stupid irreducible balks my quarrying?
Our opposite provinces in thought are levelled
I would lay my hand frank and quick on your cheek

What nets between make our looks shifty?
Our sin of the same nature and connivance.
And living in the worst of each, we must invest
A third power a mechanic ambassador of our best and most
A leap in the dark from this instant to the next
Living carried to enjoyment over.
Imperious actual, I have no means
Of gathering you away from you
Unless I fall back on my voracious tower.

I might fly from these purlieus of machine forests
White-waxed and festered at the roots by bellowing sperm
I might fly to the Sassanian empire and mould in the
margin
Like an old train among the gay weeds of a sidetrack
It will probably be in America this time perhaps Buenos
Aires
I dreamt once of Buenos Aires curved
Like a gold worm in its garden of waves of chrysanthemum.

Tower O my subduer Tower my tyrant
Loosen your girders I will become one I will conform
Girders are lovable they are like nubile girls bending
Backwards in arcs asleep when smiles are flush with their
lips
Smiles risen goldfish through currents of dreaming, tower
girded and pliant

Passed by the ancestors of GOBINEAU
Round the corners in ambush, opium touts
I am by my acceptance reassured
Saying I come! as if a voice asked Will you come?
Exultant with assent, words gay words irresistible
Moving with the Amazon's muted thunder and the crushed

humming of its songs its birds
To find its place in the sea, I can find my place.
And now I know my mind I'll sleep it off
I slip on the greased keel of sleep into the cove
Whose water cuffs my temples with plectrum taps.

I am awake pushing streams of water
Over a celluloid slate on a little table
Such as one teaches at, breaks bread, drinks wine
The four horizons are hung with a filmy curtain
It is the figures of men and women
Matrons and seniors, forked and silly maidens
Whose hope or fear death has fooled as life
And the gentle curves of cheek and hip and breast
Distinguished once by the sun have sunk away.
My hands that sweep
The lingering matchflares of the talked-out day
Are looked upon as celebrating bonfires
The dessicated mouths the eyes of reproachful prayers
Hunger and thirst the anger of blood the distress of the
heart
Attend and I declaim that I BABEUF
BABEUF and I mixed like the play of mirrors
Make *table rase* ready for primary needs
Their mouth's tense bows relieve them, releasing fingers
Their eyes bulge like gates opening
Of fortresses at morning full of prisoners
Insisting on promised deliverance.

My tower strong swimmer breasts the clouds
Warning me that fruits only follow
Skies anxious with rain and dreary furrows
And before men become dignified
Being not such as light but passes through

By accident like prisms that depend
On a stray hand
But rather their idea operative in them like health
Interluminant with their perfect each:
There has to be give for take although that sweated labour
Make us spit at the pictures of heaven we have painted
At the merchant of honour granting will with sanctions
Therefore let us bare our hold, let us
Offer our passion to the tentacular sadist
There is just one chance we dare not miss this chance.

Even then O Dilatory O You that cease,
In that town where the passages of tenderness
Are so impulsive and so expert
That the charmed inhabitants moving
With the light-sprung southwest wind's annunciation
Provoke milk-drowsy earth to flower everywhere,
Will untraced echoes not bewilder sound?
And light twitch like the wing of a drying bird?
And why of course your voice, Blood-opiate, speak?
Ah yes and demented tongues grow white
Railing at that piebald natural day
For that its inhabitants fine-limbed and content
Strut in a day blind from its own glare:
Pride of destruction of its secular enemies
Cripples and bickering and web-footed want:
Nevertheless the security of day is precipitous
The world's blatant glare merely hoods us
From dissolute mortal violence
And self-sufficiency is evil while
The dead, our true enemies, are silent.

Tower, that snowy steel town though postulant
Of full conscience and its confetti of laughter blown about

In the main street of the sun, then
Summoned when the trestle-blether texts of poverty are
irrelevant
What can it offer
More than the pretty tinkling of snowy steel?
Anything will dislocate the riveting:
A boy embittered when summer rain smells fresh on hot
limbs and
Desire trapped in a girl's wet hair breathes
Or a bored mechanic polishing and he mutters
Caught by sight of his face in one of a million rollers
Or the bewilderment of the strong and fair covertly noting
A beloved forehead suave as styles of maize becoming
Restless and stained
Or no news yet from emigrant sons:
For compromise with love defiles youth ever
Content is hollow and vile it will remain
To suffer branding from tools, the senses' servants

Farewell and good to the dead leave us reproached;
And though pain be gone still the unnoticed jungle rain of
duration patters
With maniac successive steps tramples down;
Anything we know too well or not,
The worm of anguish in the innocent heart,
Anything will startle again that voice
Shrouded in the stone dream of doom

Behind me lies the wife of my tomb, the sea
And in front the land lit up for evening.
Tower that support my view erect
Firm beneath my picture of you, stand
Let BABEUF fade; day not enough but day and night also,
now night slants

My brothers and my sisters
Shambled through the magdalanian gloom
So near the indifferent beginning that
When night threw up her hair they were her neck
Not long ago, we are fragile, in need of precept.
Tower, graph of the mind and the hand
How the hand has embraced the mind in you!
Graceful result of faith right by a hair's breadth
Mounting resolution of awry steel
Be my exemplar of the hero
Who grasps his strength with bolts, obeys and only seems
  to sway
When the bad weathers drive.

I am crowded round by the speechless amoeba-night
Massed silkworms nuclear of centuries
Days after and days after to-morrow.
Night my pure identity that breathe
One in all breaths, absorber of all breaths
Night that gestate in symbol-troubled women,
Dumb breeders of being
Wombed in your cathedrals let us watch
Till the forgotten matutinal colours flame
Various the rosewindows through
Tongues of the moon, refresh them in their labour
The stretched and willing mouths of the supple earth
Buttress-arched conceiving in sleep
Teach us the acid experience of the dead
Their diffident primaeval welcome
Persuasive Night
Drug the tigers of desire that prowl at large
That in tranquillity gradual our value flower
Like the young gawky trees
Which they would crush

Night O Clearer than the day
Because the objects of love are visible.

The people look for new commands, uncertain
Like a mother covering her ears
When the last son slams the door and she cowers from its
   echoes
I am made to speak:
   "The losses that I count will be unpleasant
   On the hither side of light for a long time
   Your looks will not leap
   The excited escarpments of colour
   Nor the broken geometry of shape
   You will lend no more to laughter
   There will be no grief each for his own grief
   But only narrow beds and milk and bread

   One thing to comfort us

IN SOME 8 YEARS."

Entry of Multitudes into an Eternal Mansion

Each time a hindrance! I, storm-inherent
Gripped in the nervous violins of their arms
    Of the Fates of Ignorance
    And Solitude milkless
Against whom I strive with these gold legions,

In spite of each failure horrifying our march
In a senseless moment outside heat and cold,
    Behold charming
    That star-crouched mansion:
Come on Come on They'll have to let us pass!

I am thrilled to scorn of the icy slabs of pain:
The Fates like an envious plebs would insulate us but
    What hurts me helps me
    And Fates are invented
Phantoms, nor like tigers carnal vibrant nor cared for.

The lightnings of their hair are whipped out
Open the doors for any love's sake! Open
    To the invading canvas
    Of harbourfuls of hands, the
Darkness resilient is pressed from the slow-lit rooftops.

Conscience at last my scaffolding high in wind!
Be nest of passage for distressed birds
    When I've won nigh you
    We'll be open to highcomers
From the rarefied clean rain whistling sweet-willed horizons.

Already be glad how with electric look

One weak torchlight, we have cut through.
    No more wet limbs
    Nor handkerchief limp
After regretted mistresses. Smash the windows

How bright our heads laced in blood mantillas!
The price for worth is shame in pain enjoyed
    You seem calm, yet
    Creation, my ferment,
Wounds throb in your nubian flesh, Night!

Primitive days in clouds of fat stank.
O caballeros caballeros hands
    Gnashing with race, fall on
    The gross canaille still stalling
In thoughtless lust the doors to the Common One

Sweetness of blood's vague way across
The bland white plains of operating tables!
    I am well in, loose me
    From these hags these futile
Visions and discourse and the pomp of signs

I demand silence from the arbitrary
That may be ordered what is going to happen
    Crowd work Shock troops
    The first communion!
O clapping hands, desist! the doors fly open.

Est Prodest

Tablelands of ice
Bastions of blocks of light
Are his identity
Or light as flutenotes
At a flick he is round me flowing
Denying, promising,
Boulders of ice, gentian,
Dazing dominant
As a tower drags up the eyes.
Whose eyes will not flare
Jerked out of sloth by sudden
Bugles and flags blaring?
In gentleness who not answer
The shy friendly nudging
Of that insistent stallion?
He stamps there, desperate, sweet,
The air aches with our breath
He is me otherwise.

If One they all say
Shows himself in us
Groups of men and women
Mnemonic said of Eden
That stink high in our nostrils
Rich and poor and dead
Then how darkly he
Is broken among us
In frosty slopes at hazard,
Sunlight on the frangent
Mirrors of the sea.

Phrases twisted through other,
Reasons reasons disproofs
Phrases lying low
Proving invalid that reason
With which I prove its truth
Identity obscured
Like the reflections of
One mirror in another,
Reasons reasons disproofs.

Ah, Numberless and Nameless
As mute walls of ivory:
Here question's waste of time.
In extreme pain, painless
The beloved and secure
The clouted sobbing fools
Are stunned in his sleep of thunder
Success or no success
Equal in effortless death:
But days by days are numbered
He must be proved in time.

Getting away with love
Drylipped love that takes
No action but battens
On misery its guest its prey
And if the pipes of my nerves
Steam at high tension
Is it then satisfaction?
Alas, that One which loves me
Is my bribe to imperfection,
By the muffled brain invented,
Is self-love in reflection.

Blinded between bookends
Cramped between streetends
I am blown blown gone foolish
This lung-exhalation
Of now impotent angels
Is useless to usage.

Here but if here I trample
On the gross hide of earth
With multitudes trampling
Then from what's superfluous
To its cause in other's agony
I am sweated into worth
We are all other's work
He being is freed moving
Seeing and seen in mirrors
We move into being,
O miracle moved like children
Tempestuous blood soothing;

And deep to my heart whisper
The charged rippling starfields
Murmur of holy cities
The maned azure whinneying
Its voices, panic
Cataracting, bestial
Breathing beyond my hearing,
Do whirl me off with gold
Serpents and seas and insects
The loosened universe flowing
Loathsome limpid, there
Shines the eternal horror.

Gaiety and filth of birth!

Bodies grip, eyes' angles
Intersect the multiplicate netting
Of lives distinct and wrangling
Each knot all other's potential
Friction and spark seminal
Of elders and outlanders.

Mirrors flashing each other
That's the only proof
Let there be no absence
The only solution
Is the flash between mirrors
Not one but many but many
Reason enough to go on with
And to bind in rough union
For combing the suspect splendours
Love enough is enough.

So come on, old slacker,
Will of all our making
In whom I grow tactic
Of presence craving
To speak in my action.

Frightened antinomies!
I have wiped example from mirrors
My mirror's face and I
Are like no god and me
My death is my life's plumed gnomon
As a bride's embrace cruciform
Reckless antinomies
Your asymptotic gasps
Have no hold on me
Now this fit is on me

And sealed mouths ripping
Tinctured with immediate
Usage which will agree to
No leave of absence
Let out their spate of birds

O fillers in of gaps!
Pure winged linking
To that which reflects me
The third from the twain distinct not
Is love of me in action.

His cliffs of ice are melted,
Lord, thy wind with pollen!
Green land, be lilied with springs!
Where now my enemies? Gadflies
Dispersed. Favouring wind,
In your muttering silken fans
Winnowing the sundust, bring him.
Lord of delight and absence
Thy bastions of light are taken
And our eyes like jewelled subtle
Fish in thee are native
Lord of light shattered
Gathered now in my breast
Lord consubstantial
My pelican-brood my pleasure!

And sky is of his breath
With what tender pressure
He breathes his sky!

And there are movements
The movements of a music

Whose sound I hear not

Tears from the depths tears
Desire glints in the peaks!
Groups of men and women
Let existence lie female
To our crystal showers, his mirrors
Till heaven over earth we shape it
Into his cognation

And he will move breathing
Through us wing-linked
Proleptic of what Eden

Quiet blown in air
Lightened as if we were

Music shall find breathing
Its breath our movement, his
Music find its breath.

Argument with Justice

Virtue all men stand under, what wonder, blinded on thy
  column transcendental, thou art
Sterile since not bedded with man thy secular wooer who
  could waken thy
Dreams to bloom; and why blinded?
Darest not take, not take to thy sight these anarchic, thy
Realms of thy reign abandoned?

Anchorite of the aether, thy influence in the brain quivers
  but tenuous . . . with what desperate antennae, dearest
  and thy
Lamps in our breast fret out, no less does thy bruised
  forehead anger us like the
Great limed birds, Isaiah and Chartres in the
Pensioner hold of thy sisters, cold heraldic
Mercy and Charity sour-dugged.

Widowed of our seed which would leaven and make serial
  thee marmoreal in the hangings of heaven, welcoming
Nature's moan as an ever imminent epithalamium, know
  that, hooded, thy
Dream of will's no will flowering in
Action, blowzed menstruate, wasting till some fancied
Excellence fit thy arrival.

Rigid, breathless to scare not thy death-heeled steps, O
  novice, we should wait thee, as pure and dawnlit, thy
Guardians, the elder cliffs of the first country to chant and
  entemple thee
Born beside an unstrung blue
Sea and trembling its transparence in thy mien, O equable!

O crags and crushed-foam beauty!

Beautiful named because from time abstract and therefore
sacrosanct? Ah, what good if the
Cunning have bandaged thee thus with eternity, turned
thee lodestar blandishing them and the
Innocent in the ignorant ruin of
Kingdoms and fevered republics babbling dry-lipped
Beneath thy blind silence?

Blown, see, against thy portals, centuries of mortals mouth
blasphemy righteous: "What reward for
Fasting, and why, the future clasped, must the present ring
of diverse winds puff out in
Vanity? She will not come down
Lest our contentment then should prove her jealous
Heaven untrue." Virtue

Virtue of all men, fear not that we thy temple crumble, flesh
crumbles but
Not till the mind's raped out. Fear rather thy name be
forgotten from father to
Son or by thy saints. Come down, let there be
Justice though the heavens fall, be virtue of our
Temporary measure.

THE LANCET

Brilliant fierce eagles
And goldfinches asleep.

Lips to drink and instruments for singing
Tight hedgerows gripped the fields now loose and drowsed
I moved about in the dark, all was quiet
The skies swollen with unshed thunder
Along the clay path my footsteps
Ominously, softly counted time.

Everyside are spread the fruitful plains
Villages live and die
Beneath the million-citied sap, the indifferent fosterage
Of trees; bloom of night
As the bloom of black grapes to your nocturnal sky
So I am near to freedom.

Now and then a shout floats up
In the court
Where the colleagues
Are drinking and musing. None
Will propose an enigma.

Look straight into my eyes when you drink: yes
The same enchantment as ever makes me yours

Your hair dims
I narrow my eyes to slits and I see
Gold copes gliding
The marketplaces foaming with white smocks
Cantilenas of men and women chained and chanting
Each mouth fabulous

With its proper version.

I have been held back
From acts of particular kindness
I have skulked in the halls of anger
And with meanness have blighted
The blossom of generous givers

But make it that I tremble
In babylon choirs, in sonorous congregation
The celebration of belled buildings,
And turn by turn stare without terror on
The rapt ravelling and unravelling of tidal generations
In which I am born and give birth and die
And above that sea
Simple and full the sun.

The drinkers topple over
Come, we are still asleep
Avoid the lunar marshes

Darkness slips
From my face, your voice
Clamours in my blood
The same enchantment as ever
The drowsy head
Dishevelled falls on my shoulder
The streams in their beds
Never tire of habit
The same enchantment
Ebony doors open, my love
Is unfulfilled, yield.
The brothers of the sun, the eagles
Are fixed among the wavering skies, yield
Bear fruit of me.

UNCOLLECTED EARLY POEMS AND TRANSLATIONS

Prayer to Our Lady, from Le Ardonnel

I

The enervating dusk; then evening
Itself is dying: noiselessly as death,
Filling the fev'rish air with burning breath,
Glides night upon us, an insidious thing.

II

That we be not empoisoned by her hate,
O stary-mantled Virgin succour us,
O Mother merciful, miraculous,
Who crushed the Serpent! O Immaculate!

III

Dreams and forgetfulness and quiet sleep
Send down to us in benediction;
Let not the crawling thing of night, icon
Of the world's evil, through our senses creep.

IV

May he fall back to depths of sombre Hell,
The serpent jealous of man by Christ redeemed,
The subtle foe o' the dark, the same that schemed
Sad ages since when Eve and Adam fell.

V

And so till morning, guarded, dangerless,

To the world's sorrows we shall close our eyes,
Then, the heart strengthened for the battle, rise
Erect at dawn, with joyous spring, and bless

VI

Thee, holy Virgin, Purity most white,
Surpassing lilies and snow-capped hill-peaks,
While shall be visible to him that seeks
The flashing image of thy Son, all-bright.

O Paltry Melancholy

O paltry melancholy —
Not of the Magdalen; her body sang with delight
Standing beneath the Cross, her once chapped white
lips red with blood kissed from the feet of Christ.
She raised her arms to Him: and her sorrow was speechless
in savage exultation; her sorrow was her salvation.

Not of Orpheus; he made of string and wood
an instrument he plucked and there was music.
Unhappy Eurydice ah! he called,
Eurydice faint down the banks of the river, Eurydice,
unwinding into the subterranean silence
of the dark Oebrian flood.
His sorrow was the silver sorrow of the poets
that bends o'er its own pain embracingly.

Not of Deirdre; she drank voluptuously
the hot and wrathful blood of Naoise, her slain Lord.
Fierce was her sorrow; measured ecstasy
swaying her golden-fleshed body
from warm throat poured the keen.

Not even the sorrow
of the lioness; she has wound over many hills
all the long night; the stars are intimate and cold,
querulous are her whines in the leafy gloom
questing her stolen cubs; at last
she stretches her brown body on the earth
and now and again
her nose moves to right and to left hoping still
to catch a fetid and dear smell on a puff of wind.

O paltry melancholy,
dragging a songless boredom through sunless and stormless days
images firing his brain of never accomplished tasks
disarming smile of humility hiding coward delays
on tiptoe in dreams beside action, sophister strutting in masks
of laughter, of childlike pagan of curled-lipped polished doubt,
a timid traveller trailing slow steps about and about
considering which route he shall take at the crossing of ways.

Before Lepanto: The Turkish Admiral Speaks to His Fleet

I

O ships!
Before us once again the sullen seas
and clamorousness of winds about the prow
and foam-fleckt stars that pin waves on the brow
of Night in storms; and laggard day that sprawls
where aftermath of sluggard loam
crawls—

II

O many ships!
Great is my grief to call you from your home
of tranquil harbours ringed with flowered quays
and age-pink malls
where white-beard merchants muse in silken ease.

III

Old watch-dogs half-asleep
how as you creep
fumbling your way over the narrow bar
I know O ancient ships
the pluméd youngsters swaggering to war
with sunlight dripping from fawn sails, and hulls
populous with wheeling crying gulls.
Then was my hand sure on the tiller, then . . .
O rhythmic swinging scimitar
time was time was . . .
Come, put on youth again
Do you hear, O fleet
a rumour crepitating o'er the sea!
That's Christian cannon crackling. Do you hear

IV

(Sudden my stale sense
vivid with light of Heaven's recompense . . .
vibrant my ear
with fretted notes that fall
from houris' fingers twanging lutes in the sun
by noise of streams, jasmin-bordered, that run
in miles of murmuring song.
O clarid streams, make musical, make musical
with measured swaying the dusky golden feet
of the blessed four that I shall rest among
answer their voices' sinuous moist call
with sweet
answering. O warm arms, drowsy lips.)

V

O westering ships!
This is the last of all
My conflicts, my last salutation
To earth and ocean and their progeny
Therefore let us put on
Brave show with ordered deck and flapping pavilion.

Loaded are we with wiles and victory
Let us go down. We have no hopes or fears,
Fate has kind subtle eyes and life prevails.

Come, brother ships, be comforted, for see
In benediction of your travailed years
The evening spreads fair sunlight on your sails.

ADAM'S HOUSE

This is the house that Adam built . . .

I cannot understand you when you say
That you are praying God because of me,
That I am incense sweetening your way,
Smothering your decay with purity.

Stinkarum, stankarum, buck . . .

The forest's full of murmurings and streams,
The pool's black wavelets creamed with froth reluce,
Beneath blue numerous leaves cold moonlight streams
On moss-embedded gleaming limbs diffuse

Of sleeping hamadryads mixt with fauns,
Brown Pan yawns, mutters, drops his flute and snores.
The gods are playing on eternal lawns
But kindly mortals sleep on fronded floors.

Stinkarum, stankarum, buck,
The old Scholastics say
That the body is filth and muck . . .

Still you have furtive eyes and coward tears,
Why should you fear the things you cannot know?
Impotent we can but tell the years
Cover you with my hair; 'tis better so.

Stinkarum, stankarum, buck,
The old Scholastics say
That the body is filth and muck
And will be dust one day.

Pool,
Lilac fringed, frog-plopping,
Slewthering moist naiads
Among tall fluted reeds.
Cool water, ah freshness
And ah, to a soul parched
Freshness of you, immobile,
Netted in moving shadow
Of waving, silent foliage
And my heart

Not sure of future anguish
Was a linnet singing in branches
To the rain-drop on your lip's corner
To the slumbrous glooms in your eyes

Riddle-me, riddle-me, rin
Why do skeletons grin? . . .

The years slipped from my shoulders
Like life from a new-born spirit.
I rose from the dark pit of the putrefaction of the heart,
and of the desolation of the broken will and the deflected
purpose.
The crapulous faces of my evil deeds
Whirled in the fumes of the pit leeringly,
And then dissolved in the sun;
My decay was asperged by your grace,
Immersed in your purity.
This is the term, I said,
To labour and groping pain,
This is the bright-fired hostel
After the tenebrous journey

Riddle-me, riddle-me, rin
Why do skeletons grin?
There is no rest on the journey . . .

O cold voice when you called
Of sirens singing in the morning winds,
And I drew near in worship; and as when
Just men are gathered quiet in a room
And silence slowly throbs with souls; so silence
Impregnate throbbed with consciousness of us.

Your hair was round my eyes
The grisping silence filled
With light notes soft as milk
Of hundred harps and flutes.

Riddle-me, riddle-me, rin
Why do skeletons grin?
There is no rest on the journey,
And death is the wages of sin.

I've had my lesson again; I might have known
Love is no talisman to the mystery.
About my ears the trumpets strong are blown
Of vengeful angels. O the little cry
Of drowning man in the night at the eleventh hour
The lamp is shattered on the perilous tower
That guards the blessed port of Paradise
And round the waste of waters and the skies
Only the carrion flap with whuling cries.

Experience teaches, you know.

Now

I

The Urn of the Occident is filled
And the blue-flamed serpent is coiled around its base,
And Pallas' bird, fixed in the sepia sky
Moveless as marble, spreads her iris wings.
Patient and proud mirroring of reality;
Arrogant gathering of sense and movement and passion
To interpret to men the profoundest soul of a man
Disgust and tire like a long drawn-out farewell
The Good no longer enfevers the sons of Plato,
Pure white and azure sky
The Hymn to Beauty is no longer chanted
Dull cold and ivory Aphrodite.

II

Eternally emerald pastures of Ireland; English lanes winding
One-ery, two-ery.
Through smothering blossom; old book shops in Paris;
Ziccary zan
Larks singing in Sussex and Deirdre's now bloodless lips.
Hollow-bone, crack-a-bone.
Vines in Avignon rich-smell charged, and brown men of Connaught.
Ninery-ten.
Honour redeemed through war; Humanity's progress
Spittery-spot.
Sweet things of home; Wanderlust tightening the throat.
Eleveny-twelve.
White hands like peace of the woman who loves me, warm

palm of my friend,

Tweedle dum-Twadle dum.

O Bridges, O Belloc, O Blunden, O Chesterton, Yeats;
O La Mare!

Diggery-delve.

III

One-ery, Two-ery
Ziccary zan . . .
Let us be Anarchists by all means
How many miles is it
Dethrone the Verb and the Substantive
To Babylon.
Roses do not smell sweeter than beans
Babylon.
Hail to the Holy Adjective!
Three-score and ten.
What's beauty, truth, life, love, what's me?
Can we get there?
Don't know, don't know, don't know.
By candle-light?
Pull down that gilded rubbish. We
Candle-Light.
In metaphysic, apotheo —
How many miles is it?
— sise Adjective. Hail Sitwell. We
How many?
Feed on our own decrease.
Can we get there . . .
One-ery, two-ery,
Ziccary zan . . .

IV

The Urn of the Occident is filled
And waits for the Embalmer.
The blue-flamed serpent is coiled around its base,
And Pallas' bird, fixed in the sepia sky
Moveless as marble, spreads her iris wings.
The green moon and the mauve sun dead in the sepia sky
And the orange grass attend the Embalmer.
Let him come, smooth-paced, urbane
Let him impose resigned hands on these rich ashes
Of the Tuscans and of the Castilians
Of Weimar
Of England and of France
All is here in these rich-smelling ashes
And when the Embalmer, vague, decadent,
Such hands shall have imposed,
Let him go.
His eyes are of desolation,

How many miles is it?

Like a cat's eyes in the dark window of a lighted chamber.

To Babylon.

The world is sudden a medium grey; and he beholds

Can we get there . . . ?

Quick hypnotised, the wooden hobby horses
Roundabout roundabout roundabout round
Roundabout roundabout roundabout round.

Can we get there . . .
One-ery, two-ery,
Ziccary . . .
Roundabout roundabout roundabout . . .

Passerelle

TRANS. BONHEUR

Pris dans l'orage des chevelure
fauché par les cordes des bras
gisant au bas des étages rocheux
enflés de drames
(ouvrez la porte pour l'amour)
gisant au bas des falaises qu'assaillent
les bâtards baveux de la mer
coeur
échafaudage de vent
où s'abritent parfois les oiseaux de passage
regarde
comme il a suffi d'une lampe
pour venir à bout de cette broussaille
regarde la fenêtre en mantille de sang
On blesse ta chair nubienne Nuit
Souvent je me suis penché sur mes papiers
pour des ratures des caresses
A quoi bon
Les jours gardaient un relent de pomme rance
Mais maintenant
o caballeros caballeros mains
vous avez foncé sur la canaille
et voilà qu'une voie incertaine saigne
à travers les plaines blanches des tables d'opération
Plus de mouchoirs flasques
plus de membres moites
plus de phrases en suspens
plus de regrets sur les pancartes récentes
L'arbitraire se taira
et j'ordonnerai le futur
Cessez la claque, ô mains
Les portes s'ouvrent

THE INVESTITURE OF D'ARTAGNAN

Crimson, diamonds and black eyebrows, trees no rough
  Spring rescinds.
I am still lorded by these red-heeled bucks with bird brains.
My cloak falls indolently as theirs, O my ragged cranes
Reproach me from the shy rectitude of our grey Biscayan
  winds.

With you is my last dignity in retreat from these the precise
  great.
By Clio squandered, I have pacted with the times unworthy
  of my chance,
Embroidered, twirling a feckless baton, first marshal
  of France
Who should have ridden the times in spasm, have been
  I the State.

Bitter to take. Bitter to get all except my will, foiled feeder:
My epoch's weaned too soon. How the Emperor pounded
  provinces cutting through
The obedient mammals that barely tumble above clay and
  spew ...
Some other age jagged into fear waits to fulfill its Leader.

Everything else. Faces light up and eyes when I come near.
Bow my burgher, Condé had not such honour, the armies
  so in nature
Personal with me, they love me not like a conscious creature
Rather as the ocean reflects the whim of the sky in
  spontaneous fear.

Most men fret for such love whom the saviour lighthouse

solitude would drive mad:
Such like gummed to like for proof of life: Which irks me for
I could mock myself into danger their laws and their laundered heart abhor,
A king-pet in lace of minuets woven while the age mends bad

Foreclosed. Not to be captain-conqueror of kneaded minds is my gift
To resignation, smile to the King, Sire I cannot leave
These lawns the hereditary breezes bevel, this soft life a reprieve
From my intended life. . . Remember on the last mountain drift

Of snow in May, the depths, insects and birds cried in birth, the breeze
Freshened the streams and as the whole blue sky opened, my
Plumes beat the sun, I swung my cold sword and screeched, I
D'ARTAGNAN flushed among a flurry of eagles in the Pyrenees!

SHE OF ALWAYS, ALL OF HER, FROM ÉLUARD

If I say to you: "I have abandoned everything"
It is that she is not my body's she,
I have never bragged about it,
It is not true
And the ground-swell fog where I move round
Never knows if I have passed.

Fan of her mouth, reflection of her eyes,
I am the only one to talk of them,
I am the only one to be surrounded
By this mirror so null where the air moves on through me
And the air has a face, a beloved face,
A loving face, thy face,
To thee that hast not any name and whom no other knows,
The sea says: on me, the sky says: on me,
The planets guess, the clouds imagine thee
And the blood shed at the best moments,
And the blood of generosity
Carries thee with delight.

I sing the great joy of singing thee,
The great joy of having thee or of not having thee,
The candour of awaiting thee, the ignorance of knowing
thee,
O thou that suppressest forgetfulness, hope and ignorance,
That suppressest absence and that I put in the world
I sing for singing's sake, I love thee for singing
The mystery in which love creates me
And is of itself delivered.

Thou are pure, more pure even than myself.

Nakedness of Truth, from Éluard

Despair has no wings,
Nor love either,
No face,
They speak not,
I stir not,
I look at them not,
I speak to them not
But I am quite as living as my love and my despair.

Girls in Love, from Éluard

They have high shoulders
And a bold gay air
Or else faces that bewilder
Trustfulness is in their breast
High up where the dawn of their breasts rises
To unclothe night.

Eyes to break pebbles
Smiles without advertence
For each dream
Storms of cries of snow
Lakes naked
And shadows rooted up.

They must be believed on a kiss
On a word on a look
Only their kisses are to be kissed

I show nothing except your face
The great storms of your throat
All I know all I am ignorant of
My love thy love thy love thy love thy love.

ONE FOR ALL, FROM ÉLUARD

One or several
The azure sleeping on the storm
The snow on the birds
The noises of fear in the peevish woods

One or several
Ravens have been sown in the shells of the clay
On faded wings on the beak of the earthquake
They have gathered the fantastic russet roses of the storm

One or several
The lace collar of the sun
The immense strawberry of the sun
On the bottle-neck of a glade

One or several
More sensitive to their childhood
Than to the rain and fine weather
Gentler to know
Than the gentle slope of sleep
Far from spleen

One or several
In teasing mirrors
Where their voice at morning is ripped like linen

One or several
Made of frittering stone
And of dispersing feathers
Made of thorns made of linen of alcohol of foam
Of laughter of sobs of negligence of ridiculous anxieties
Made of flesh and real eyes doubtless

One or several
With all their faults all their merits merits
Women

One or several
Face gloved with ivy
Tempting as fresh bread
All the women that move me
Adorned with that which I have wished
Adorned with calm and freshness
Adorned with salt with water with sun
With tenderness with boldness and with a thousand caprices
With a thousand chains

One or several
In all my dreams
A new flower of the woods
A barbarian flower with pistils like faggots
In the bruised night

One or several

A youth to die of
A youth violent unquiet and brimmed with spleen
Which she has shared with me
Without caring about the others.

They are Alike, from Éluard

I change my mind
Following the breezes of fine thread
Following your legs your hands your eyes
The subtle dress which invents you
For you to replace it.

I change my mind
You pass in the street
In a hurricane of sun
I meet you I stop
I am young you must remember

I change my mind
Your mouth is absent
I speak to you no longer you are asleep
There are fires of terror in your night
A field of clear tears in your dreams
We are not sad together
I forget you.

I change my mind
You cannot sleep
On careless ladders
Interminably
Between the flower and the fruit
In space
Between the flower and the fruit
You seek sleep
The first hoar frost
And you forget me.

I change my mind
You laugh you are living you play
And curious one a desert would people itself
  for you
And I have trust.

Finished
I have never been able to forget you
We shall never leave each other
To security we must give
The peasant snow the millstone of ruins
A respectable death
The day in pure loss drowns the stars
On the point of a single look
Of the same contemplation
We must burn the sphinx that resembles us
And its seasonable eyes
And its mosses of solitude.

The Vertebrate Sphinx, from Breton

The beautiful shadow patient and bent makes the round of the pavements
The venetian windows open and close on the square
Where firefollowed beasts go in freedom
The wet streetlamps rumble framed in a cloud of blue eyes
Which load the landscape up above the town
This morning prow of the sun how thou art swallowed up in the lofty chants given out in the old style behind the curtains by the naked spy-girls
While the giant arum lilies turn about their waist
And the mannequin bleeding jumps on her three feet into the granary
He comes they say rearing their neck where leaping plaits liberate glaciers barely pink
Which split beneath the weight of a lightray falling from ripped-off windowblinds
He comes it is the wolf with glass teeth
He that eats the hour in little round boxes
He that blows the too-piercing perfumes of the grasses
He that smokes the little passing fires at evening in the turnips
The columns of the great marble and vetiver apartments cry
They cry they are taken with these movements of coming and going which constituted till then the animation only of certain colossal factory rooms
The women motionless on revolving plates are going to see
It is day to the left but night completely night to the right
There are branchclusters still full of birds passing at top speed and darkening the crossroads hole
White birds that lay black eggs
Where are those birds whose place is now taken by stars

edged with two rows of pearls
A fishhead very very long it is not yet he
The fishhead gives birth to maidens shaking a sieve
And from the sieve to hearts made of batavian tears
He comes it is the wolf with glass teeth
He that overflew so high the vague grounds that had appeared again above the houses
With sharpened plants all turned towards his eyes
So green as to challenge a mossy bottle overturned on the snow
His jade claws in which he is mirrored in flight
His skin the colour of sparks
It is he that grumbles in the smithies at twilight and in the cast-off undies
He is visible you can touch him he advances with his scales on the wire stretched with swallows
The spy-girls lean and lean out the windows
With their whole side of shadow their whole side of light
The spool of day is pulled jerk by jerk towards the sand paradise
The pedals of night stir without interruption

The Plume, from Breton

If only the sun were to rise to-night
If two bright mirrorglittering breasts in the depths of the Opera
Were to make a most wonderful living letterbox for the word LOVE
If the wood pavement had its opening in the mountaintops
If the erminefowl would look beseechingly
At the priest with red headbands
Coming from jail and counting the closed cars
If the rich echo of the streams which I torment
Pitched my body alone to the weeds of Paris
Would there were hailstorms inside the jewel stores
Then at least Spring would scare me no more
If only I were a root of the tree of heaven
The Good at last in the sugarcane of the air
If one were giving women the heave-up
What seest thou beautiful silent one
Beneath the Triumphal Arch of Carrousel
If pleasure in the guise of a perpetual passer-by were in control
The Government Buildings furrowed in future only by the violent glad-eyes of the promenades
What wouldn't I give for an arm of the Seine to slide under the morning
Which is lost in any case
I am not resigned either to the petting halls
Where the telephone rings at evening to make it up
On leaving I set fire to a lock of hair which is that of a bomb
And the lock of hair digs a tunnel under Paris
If only my train would go in to that tunnel

Allotropy, from Breton

The electric bell rings again
Who's that coming in
It's me pull yourself together if you want me to recognize
  you
The chest is full of linen
There are even moonrays which I can unfold
You have changed
Here is proof that you have changed
The gifts one makes to the dead in their coffin
The gifts one makes to the newborn in their cradle
Are almost the same the arrow points the direction whence
  you come
Where you go
Your heart is on the route of that arrow
Your eyes about to be bright again are filled with the fog of
  things
Your hands on tipfinger along a railway seek out the dark
  needle to ward off the disaster
You see the women you have loved
Without their seeing you you see them without their seeing
  you
As you have loved them without their seeing you
The black wolves pass in their turn behind you
Who are you
Shadow of an evildoer on the great walls
Shadow of a signalman going past the signal
I am the guilty principal guilty
The principal innocent at the same time
My head rolls from above there where my steps will never
  carry
What a make-up

No one will recognize me
Later among the stones caving in
Bend down
Bend down to change again
It sure is you that bend down and change
This photograph you forgot to have developed
It's you all right

Rather Life, from Breton

Rather life than those prisms with no density even if their
 colours are purer
Rather than that ever covered hour than those terrible
 coaches of cold flames
Than those bletted stones
Rather this heart with its notch for stopping
Than that mere with its murmurs
And than that white stuff singing at the same time in the air
 and in the earth
Than that nuptial blessing uniting my forehead with the
 forehead of total vanity
Rather Life

Rather life and its trick conjurer cloths
The scars of its evasions
Rather life rather this rosewindow on my grave
Life of presence nothing but of presence
Where a voice says Are you there or another answers Are
 you there
I am scarcely here alas
And yet even if it means playing the game of that which we
 put to death
Rather life

Rather life rather life venerable Childhood
The ribbon which starts from a fakir
Is like to the groove of the world
In vain is the sun a mere wreck
However little a woman's body is like to him
You still think when watching the trajectory all its length
Or only in closing the eyes on the adorable storm which is

named your hand
Rather life

Rather life with its waiting rooms
When we know we shall never be announced
Rather life than those hot-spring spas
Where the attendants are in neck-yoke
Rather life long and without favour
Even if books must here be closed on less gentle shelves
And even if down there it would be better than best it
would be free yes
Rather life

Rather life as a background of contempt
For this head beautiful enough
As the antidote of that perfection it calls on and it fears
Life the make-up of God
Life like a clean passport
A little town like Pont-à-Mousson
And as everything has said to itself already
Rather life

NA LEANNÁIN, FROM NERVAL

Cá bhfuil ár leannáin?
Táid fé lic na marbh:
Aoibhnede a mbeatha
Sciamhaí a n-áitreabh!

Iad le hais na n-aingeal
I ngormdoimhneas aeir,
Moladh acu is caintic
Do Mháthair Mhic Dé!

A óigh óigh fé bhláthacht!
A chailín fhinn ion-nuachar!
A leannáin do fágadh
Is go meathann tú fé chian . . .

Ag miongháirí in bhur súilibh
Tá an tSíoraíocht ródhomhain:
A thóirsí sa domhan do múchadh,
Ar neamh bhur n-athadhnadh!

TÓRRAMH, FROM RIMBAUD

Is é an suan fé shoiléireacht é, nach eitinn nochar laige ar an leaba nó san iath.
Is é an cara é nach áilíosach nochar fann. An Cara.
Is í an ionúin í nach céasann nochar céastar. An Ionúin.
An t-aer agus an saol nár cuartaíodh. An Bheatha.

An Áille, from Baudelaire

Chomh hálainn mé, a dhaonnacht, is líog a chífí i mbruadar,
Tagann gach n-aon im chliabh dá chneá i ndiaidh a chéile,
Mo chliabh ag taoscadh grá ina thinfeadh san éigse
Grá chomh taoitheangach is chomh buan leis an dúlra.
Táim mar sphinx fá rún im shuí san aer go ríoga
Chomh bán leis an eala is mo chroí mar shneachta ionam;
Is fuath liom an luail a chuireas líní as ionad,
Ní dheinim gáire ná ní ghoilim riamh nó choíche.

Fanfaidh éigse os comhair mo stáid is mo chumtha mórga
A fuair mé i ndealramh na gcarn cuimhne is mó mórtais
Éigse ag gabháil don staidéar géar go ceann a saoil;
Óir tá dhá bhriocht agam a mheallas an t-aos grá ciúin,
Dhá scáthán íon ag tabhairt breis áille do gach ní —
Dhá shúil, dhá shúil mhóra lán den tsoiléireacht bhuan!

Leoithne Gaoithe Muirí, from Mallarmé

Mo thrua an cholainn faraor! — do léas gach uile leabhar.
Teitheadh i gcéin! Mothaím go bhfuil éanlaith as a meabhair
A bheith idir an cúr anaithnid agus an spéir!
Faic, ná seanghairdín á dhealbhadh i súil shoiléir,
Ní choiscfidh faic mo chroí dena thumadh féin sa mhuir,
A oícheanta! ná solas fásach mo lampa
Ar an bpáipéar folamh atá á chosaint trí bheith bán,
Ná fós an bhean óg úd a oileas a naíonán.
Imeod romham! a ghaltáin ag luascadh do ghléas crann,
Tóg d'ancaire, téam go tír a mbíonn saol eile ann!
Dá uaigní mo chás de bharr an dóchais dúir
Creidim fós i mbeannacht déanach na gciarsúr!
Meallfaidh na crainn an anfa, ab'fhéidir nach bhfuil i ndán
Dóibh ach lúbadh síor os cionn long bhriste ar fán
Gan inis torrach, gan chrann, gan aon chrann dár sábháil . . .
Éist fós, a chroí, tá rann ag muirithe á ghabháil.

Amhrán an Leannáin Mhí-Ámharaigh, from Apollinaire

Tráthnóna ceoigh éadrom is mé i Londain
Tháinig cladhaire óg dom dháil
Agus gnúis air mar ghnúis mo ghrá
D'fhéach sé orm go géar am bhuaireadh
Gur dhallas radharc mo shúl ón náir.

Do chas sé suas port feadaíola
A lámha ina phóca is mé á leanadh
Ba dhóigh leat orainn idir na tithe
Gur i mbun Rua Mara scoilte a bhíomar,
Gurb é an tArm Eabhrach is mise an Forann.

Más rud nár thugas fíorghrá duitse
Más rud nach tú an t-aonghrá aonda,
Na tonnta bríce seo go dtitid!
Is mise Ardrí na hÉigipte
Is mise a sluasan is a dheirfiúr chéile.

Ag cúinne sráide a bhí tré thine
Ag uileshoilse éadan tí
Créachta an cheoigh ag sileadh fola,
Caointe ar clos ó lár an tí,
Do léim bean as tigh tábhairne amach

Agus gnúis uirthi mar ghnúis mo ghrá
Mar ba léir dom óna crot neamhdhaonna
Ón gcreáchtlorg a bhí ar a bráid
Is í ar meisce sa nóimeat céanna
Inar admhaíos féin gur bréag an grá.

Ar theacht thar n-ais don a oileán dúchais

Fé dheireadh na ndeireadh d'Uilíos eagnaí,
D'aithnigh amháin a sheanchú é
Is a bhean ag feitheamh leis do fuair sé,
Táipéis bhreá aici is í á fí.

B'aoibhinn do rífhear Sacantáile
Nuair d'éirigh tuirseach dá chathbhuaibh
Agus go bhfuair sé arís liathbhán í
A súla lag ón ngrá is ón súil
Is an fia lena taobh á bhogfháisceadh.

Thángadar i ngleic, na taibhsí neamhdhílse
Gur chuimhin liom an dá rí shéanmhar sin,
Taibhse an ghrá bhréagaigh, taibhse an tí
Go dtugaim fós grá dhi,
Is nach iad anó mo chroí istigh!

Bunús ifrinn an cumha atá orm
Neamh an dearmaid dom ghuí go n-osclaí!
Gheobhaidís bás le dúil ina póig,
Ríthe an tsaoil, na taoisigh bhochta,
Dhíolfadh a n-anamacha ina comhair.

Mé san allód im gheimhreadhshsuan
Ó! tagadh grian na Cásca ar ais
Do ghoradh mo chroí atá níos oiriúla
Ná daichead máirtir an tSebaist,
Dom ghoradh féin, táim lánbrúite.

Long bhreá is ea thú, Och, a chuimhne!
Nach leor dúinn bheith ag triall ar muir
Sa taoide atá chomh salach le n-ibhe ann
Is nach leor dúinn a bheith ar fán
Ó mhoiche lae go nóin doilíosach!

Adieu, a ghrá bhréagaigh atá dod mheascadh
Trín mhnaoi a laghdaíos a réim im chuimhne,
Tríd an té baineadh díom
Sa Ghearmáin an bhliain ghabh tharainn,
Ní fheicfidh mé go deo arís í.

A Shíog na Spéire, a dheirfiúr shoilseach
Sruthán bán Tíre Canaan
Is corp bán leannán, an leanfam inár
Snámhaithibh marbh fé lánochaíocht
Do thriall fé dhéin réaltbhuíon eile?

Is cuimhin, is cuimhin liom bliain eile
Bhí sé ina mhoiche lae Aibreáin
Chan mé mo shearc, chan mé mo shoilbhir,
De ghuth breá fir do chan mé an grá
Is an bhliain féin ar tí ionúine.

LOUGH DERG AND OTHER POEMS
(1946)

Lough Derg

The poor in spirit on their rosary rounds,
The jobbers with their whiskey-angered eyes,
The pink bank clerks, the tip-hat papal counts,
And drab, kind women their tonsured mockery tries,
Glad invalids on penitential feet
Walk the Lord's majesty like their village street.

With mullioned Europe shattered, this Northwest,
Rude-sainted isle would pray it whole again:
(Peasant Apollo! Troy is worn to rest.)
Europe that humanized the sacred bane
Of God's chance who yet laughed in his mind
And balanced thief and saint: were they this kind?

Low rocks, a few weasels, lake
Like a field of burnt gorse; the rooks caw;
Ours, passive, for man's gradual wisdom take
Firefly instinct dreamed out into law;
The prophets' jewelled kingdom down at heel
Fires no Augustine here. Inert, they kneel;

All is simple and symbol in their world,
The incomprehended rendered fabulous.
Sin teases life whose natural fruits withheld
Sour the deprived nor bloom for timely loss:
Clan Jansen! less what magnanimity leavens
Man's wept-out, fitful, magniloquent heavens

Where prayer was praise, O Lord! the Temple trumpets
Cascaded down Thy sunny pavilions of air,
The scroll-tongued priests, the galvanic strumpets,

All clash and stridency gloomed upon Thy stair;
The pharisees, the exalted boy their power
Sensually psalmed in Thee, their coming hour!

And to the sun, earth turned her flower of sex,
Acanthus in the architects' limpid angles;
Close priests allegorized the Orphic egg's
Brood, and from the Academy, tolerant wranglers
Could hear the contemplatives of the Tragic Choir
Drain off man's sanguine, pastoral death-desire.

It was said stone dreams and animal sleeps and man
Is awake; but sleep with its drama on us bred
Animal articulate, only somnambulist can
Conscience like Cawdor give the blood its head
For the dim moors to reign through druids again.
O first geometer! tangent-feelered brain

Clearing by inches the encircled eyes,
Bolder than the peasant tiger whose autumn beauty
Sags in the expletive kill, or the sacrifice
Of dearth puffed positive in the stance of duty
With which these pilgrims would propitiate
Their fears; no leafy, medieval state

Of paschal cathedrals backed on earthy hooves
Against the craftsmen's primary-coloured skies
Whose gold was Gabriel on the patient roofs,
The parabled windows taught the dead to rise,
And Christ the Centaur, in two natures whole,
With fable and proverb joinered body and soul.

Water withers from the oars. The pilgrims blacken
Out of the boats to masticate their sin

Where Dante smelled among the stones and bracken
The door to Hell (O harder Hell where pain
Is earthed, a casuist sanctuary of guilt!).
Spirit bureaucracy on a bet built

Part by this race when monks in convents of coracles
For the Merovingian centuries left their land,
Belled, fragrant; and honest in their oracles
Bespoke the grace to give without demand,
Martyrs Heaven winged nor tempted with reward.
And not ours, doughed in dogma, who never have dared

Will with surrogate palm distribute hope:
No better nor worse than I who, in my books,
Have angered at the stake with Bruno and, by the rope
Watt Tyler swung from, leagued with shifty looks
To fuse the next rebellion with the desperate
Serfs in the sane need to eat and get;

Have praised, on its thunderous canvas, the Florentine smile
As man took to wearing his death, his own,
Sapped crisis through cathedral branches (while
Flesh groped loud round dissenting skeleton)
In soul, reborn as body's appetite:
Now languisht back in body's amber light,

Now is consumed. O earthly paradise!
Hell is to know our natural empire used
Wrong, by mind's moulting, brute divinities.
The vanishing tiger's saved, his blood transfused.
Kent is for Jutes again and Glasgow town
Burns high enough to screen the stars and moon.

Well may they cry who have been robbed, their wasting

Shares in justice legally lowered until
Man his own actor, matrix, mould and casting,
Or man, God's image, sees his idol spill.
Say it was pride that did it, or virtue's brief:
To them that suffer it is no relief.

All indiscriminate, man, stone, animal
Are woken up in nightmare. What John the Blind
From Patmos saw works and we speak it. Not all
The men of God nor the priests of mankind
Can mend or explain the good and broke, not one
Generous with love prove communion;

Behind the eyes the winged ascension flags,
For want of spirit by the market blurbed,
And if hands touch, such fraternity sags
Frightened this side the dykes of death disturbed
Like Aran Islands' bibulous, unclean seas:
Pietà: but the limbs ache; it is not peace.

Then to see less, look little, let hearts' hunger
Feed on water and berries. The pilgrims sing:
Life will fare well from elder to younger,
Though courage fail in a world-end, rosary ring.
Courage kills its practitioners and we live,
Nothing forgotten, nothing to forgive,

We pray to ourself. The metal moon, unspent
Virgin eternity sleeping in the mind,
Excites the form of prayer without content;
Whitethorn lightens, delicate and blind,
The negro mountain, and so, knelt on her sod,
This woman beside me murmuring *My God! My God!*

ENCOUNTER

''Our saints are poets, Milton and Blake,
Who would rib men with pride against the spite
Of God,'' the Englishman said, and in the silence
Hatred sparkled along our bones. He said:
''Celt, your saints adorn the poor with roses
And praise God for standing still.''

Between the two of us, François from Touraine,
Where women and the wheat ripen and fall due
Suavely at evening, smiled, teasing the breadcrumbs.
He whispered: ''Patience; listen to the world's
Growth, resulting in fire and childlike water!''

And I: ''Milton and Marvell, like the toady, Horace,
Praised the men of power for the good
They happened on, with bible and sword; the wretched
Hold out their begging-bowls at the wooden gates,
Too poor to weep, too poor to weep with tears.''

Boxflower scent. Fumes of burgundy.
Nagging children at the tables
A dream's remove from their fathers smoking
Along the boulevard laid with yellow evening.

FROM GOVERNMENT BUILDINGS

Evening lapses. No pity or pain, the badgered
Great get home, and the little, tomorrow's anchorage,
All smiling, sour the milk of charity,
Like the pyrrhonist poets, Love's saboteurs.

The clerks fan out and the lamps; and I look inwards:
What turns amuse you now? with whom, not me! do
You cower in Time, whose palsied pulse is nimbler
A hair's breadth when want and have are equal?

My room sighs empty with malignant waiting;
The November wind slows down outside, wheeling
Twig and awning on the brick balcony,
A wind with hackles up. In Rome at evening

Swallows traced eggshapes on the vellum sky,
The wind was warm with blue rain in Dublin;
When the culture-heroes explored the nether world
It was voiceless beasts on the move made Death terrible.

Friendship I will not, barring you; to have witness does:
Doll birds, dogs with their social nose, by day
Are touchstone. But at night my totem silence
With face of wood refuses to testify.

The famous exile's dead, from many on many
Deportations, from Spain to Prague to Nice,
Kaleidoscopic police, his Danse Macabre;
One of the best the worst had never feared.

You, you I cherish with my learned heart

As in the bombed cathedral town, doubly
A tourist trophy now, the dean shouted: "At last!
At least and at last we have stored the windows away,

The fabulation of my Lord's glory, by
Seven and by seven and by seven multiplied!"
So is my care though none your mystic I,
Nor you like the painted saints but breath and more.

And do not pace the room haunting the future
But be my insular love; and I would have you
Fingering the ring with its silver bat, the foreign
And credible Chinese symbol of happiness.

THE STATUE AND THE PERTURBED BURGHERS

Emptied and pearly skulls
Lie humbly among the roots of the grass
The inhabitants know it only too well
Walking delicately
Under the trees.
They have stayed this fluttering boy in tight marble
For a fresh similitude
Of their rare immersion in stillness,
Planted foaming trees
For coolness.

People of worth and wealth
Glancing with care at their modes of life,
Walls, cradles, windows, amber orchards.

My watch ticks as loud as a sledgehammer in an empty
  street.
Muffle the panting hours, my fountain, disdain them,
Boy with the beaked chin.

The tendrils of fountain water thread that silk music
From the hollow of scented shutters
Crimson and blind
Crimson and blind
As though it were my sister
Fireflies on the rosewood
Spinet playing
With barely escaping voice
With arched fastidious wrists to be so gentle.

Memo from a Millionaire

What jugs, what knives, what cups for drinking in!
My keys! my watch! my silk-protected skin!
Ginger and orange glowing, mouse-foot peas,
My princely delft! my girls with deft, silk knees,
A wineglass feted on the roulette cardboard,
Thumbcurl frescoes veer, veer to starboard
While my steward, with chuckle apples, brings
My guests, whose hunger's punctual as kings,
Beautiful and casual like those masks the sun
Breaks off from burning clouds at his decline.

Take you my food and games, swear at my crew:
I am more than you by what I give to you;
If panic whirled me to unload my shares:
How would these guests convert all bulls to bears,
From their dark brokeries nag at me and nibble
Till my proud plethora crumbled to a dribble!
But better in the meantime rich and rooked
Than poor and pawned and crumb-thrifty and crocked,
Even if my only friends, like my desires,
Are doll outside but, inside, space and wires —
Joseph, that sandy baron, made his pile
In heretic Egypt, God indulged his guile:
Having it both ways, Ghibelline and Guelph?
The money's hard, I would not blame myself.

Time only blame me, Time with outlaw right,
Ambush me in my shadow-slip mind's night;
Mirror my double, merciless: a sinister
Cynical bishop in his empty minster!

"What of that youth," Time asks, "wherein you dreamt
Instruments for my meaning and measurement?
These irritating, unseen wings that force
My massive moves, you failed to chart their course."
Ah, Time, unjust! that spawn stars, keys and knives
For your imperious increase, with lives
With seaports and with ships like these, what turning
I took, what time, was of your make and earning.

I have spicked and spanned my life until it shone
Like my crisp steamer with its sunny brain.
Sun, be my shield! disturb not my agreement;
Let the rays fly as far as they are meant
Lest, in the tragic sense, a sweet breast dip
And warn young lovers life springs from a slip:
No door, no door tear out the wall with it,
My house of tricks, last out your siege in habit;
Pretend, my spectrumed ear, to tones, for show,
You cannot really catch, thread to the radio
The escaped canary in the garden tree
Practising with chill chirps a headlong spree
And the dragonfly that hums an unheard noise, as
He procreates in pretty circular poises.

Who sees me, with the dust of my possessions,
Unmoistened mortar, mending Time's abrasions?
Who knows me, lunging at a drunken sock
Jack-knifed to daylight by my cock-shriek clock
From my confessional of night, whose phantoms
Act out my stunted sainthood, twit my tantrums?
Outfoxed, forsworn, belittled and outbannered! —
If from that good despair I rise, well-mannered
To taunt my dainty guests; with tailored pride
Review my keys, my watch, my ship-flecked tide.

Royal Canal

She will stand in the window any moment now
The world plunged in the evening light
A costly silence between enemies.

The gruff mongrels in aimless exercise
With boys shouting; and then a silence.
All shouting waves around
Silence like a blind egg
Terror fills her old eyes as in girlhood

She turns from the window; her fingers
Feather the keyboard
A brush of melodies
A perspicuous storm of chords
She finishes nothing.

The druid elms, closed in their lost language,
Their shoulders heavy
With a menance not their natural own
Rest in panic on the still canal.

MIXED DRINKS

The whiskey's prurience through the inner pipes.
This is the change and leaving of thy name.

If the fungus of drunken breathing
Mist feels at the mirrors
Like doubt turning to anger
In the judge's face.

Blond beer cylinders weave
The waitresses' trays ripple over our heads.
I am alone but the others are with me
Tasting the same food, drink and sleep
After the day of ambush
When anguish made the soul efficient
With bell, book and candle,
When the lie startled like stoats into hiding
In the eyes of butcher, baker and banker,
When death put up a showy magazine front
For officer and ranker.

It is a kind of dream-desecration
Of the most beautiful forms man has imagined:
Yet you feel less defiled than when you see
The uncompetitive horror in the eyes
Of a dying man
A little before death.

A shabby-nosed old drunk
Limns with one loyal, black-gloved hand
The motions of a baton, orchestrating
Out of the oxen heart

The world, the flesh and the devil,
The dare of the trumpets, ivied erosion of theme,
Violin-shell children.

Jansenist Journey

"Then we'll go through with the journey," said
My brother and myself, "and bring
With us our black-faced scapegoat, Guilt."

We bested the last lingering hill
Of life; and got donkeys to ride
For it would be long going through the wood.

I was to loose our goat of guilt
At a shameful bypath on the way;
But the brightness turned him innocent:

The donkey's patience through the thorns,
The gay old nurses, the green inns:
He bucked the wild flowers with flashing horns:

These freshets garlic to his taste.
But I put no trust in him, no trust.
At last we reached the Gospel gates,

Aching and dirty. Robes lay there.
Mother and sisters like light through glass,
With stopped lightning stood in the arch.

They washed our heads, hands and feet,
In the same low voice they laughed and sobbed,
The mother gave us a diamond each,

Casketed, shut with a miser's clasp.
I said to my brother: "Life, the diamond,
Is locked inside hard and fast."

"Yes?" he said, putting his down
Indifferently. I opened mine:
It was a gold ball. It was sundown,

We entered cloisters with a priest,
Sat on the stone wall, listening
To his plans for our retreat,

Black-face forgotten, the diamond too,
And the mother and sisters. No rapture;
The plain virtue of the chosen few.

Casa Buonaroti

He struggled all life with pigment, rock, chisel and sun
To put God in matter, magnify himself;
Worked against Time, rhetorical skull on the shelf,
To muscle in stone ideas by Time undone:
And skull's grin, that long bogy, would outrun
His work yielded to Time: why God made Hell:
The inch to retreat to from the daring ell
Of giving his image the risk of being none.

Not devils but the meek minimize the great
Who bind their eyes as likely as not
So not is like what they would like it were.
Samson they enhance us whom our flaws deflate:
Yet God, from the refuge of his comic thought,
Moves the momentary tourist with his fear.

West Pier

The master says, Good Dog! and the mailboat
Dips for the start.
The moon's mad, sharp face extracts
From the fields an inadvertent animal wail.

Those two with head to head against the gangway,
Two as close as joined palms, if pulled apart,
Their lifeline will be stopped short and everything
Look different as at night.

Aboriginal anger and Christian terror
Wound happiness. The stevedore
Knifes his way through the port when hurt; the steward
Dims apprehension with the daily rosary,
Life and death all needled on the frail
Manipulations between boat and sea,
The balance tipped over by the slightest finger.

The land trembles like water in the green light.
Damp couples dawdle on the pier,
Their snug paradise to be a giving
And a taking away.
The wicked and the pious, driving, driven
Excuse a withered life by a useful one.

The sea's gamesome voice is seen
A quarter mile out where the promontories
Excoriate its dark glass skin
I love and lose her with an ever love.

Sleep or death, those canyons come upon
Beneath the moon's debauched, athenian smile,
Will terrify with monstrous theatre
Our anger and our terror.
                                        That screen is mist,
That screen on which you do your lives bedizen,
Two on the gangway, steward and stevedore.

Est Prodest

Tablelands of ice
Bastions of blocks of light
Are his identity
Or light as flutenotes
At a flick he is round me flowing
Denying, promising,
Boulders of ice, gentian,
Daring, dominant
As a tower drags up the eyes.
Whose eyes will not flare
Jerked out of sloth by sudden
Bugles and flags blaring?
In gentleness, who not answer
The shy, friendly nudging
Of that insistent stallion?
He stamps there, desperate, sweet,
The air aches with our breath.
He is me otherwise.

If One, they all say,
Shows himself in us
Groups of men and women
Mnemonic said of Eden
That stink high in our nostrils
Rich and poor and dead:
Then how darkly he
Is broken among us
In frosty slopes at hazard,
Sunlight on the frangent
Mirrors of the sea.

Phrases twisted throughother
Reasons reasons disproofs
Identity obscured
Like mirrors shining throughother
Reasons reasons disproofs.

Ah, Numberless and Nameless
As mute walls of ivory:
Here question's waste of time.
In extreme pain, painless
The beloved and secure
The clouted sobbing fools
Are stunned in his sleep of thunder
Success or no success
Equal in effortless death:
But days by days are numbered
He must be proved in Time.

Getting away with Love
Dry-lipped love that takes
No action, but battens
On misery, its guest, its prey:
And if the pipes of my nerves
Steam at high tension
Is it then satisfaction?
Alas, that One which loves me
Is my bribe to imperfection
By the muffled brain invented
Is self-love in reflection.

I am blown blown gone foolish
This lung-exhalation
Of now impotent angels
Is useless to usage.

Here, but if here I trample
On the gliding hides of earth
With multitudes trampling:
Then, out of what's superfluous
To its cause in other's agony,
I am sweated into worth
We are all other's work.
He being is freed moving
Seeing and seen in mirrors
We move into being
O miracle moved like children!
Distempered blood soothing;

And deep to my heart whisper
The charged, rippling starfields
Murmur of cities
The maned azure whinneying
Its voices, panic,
Cataracting, bestial,
Breathing beyond my hearing,
Do whirl me off with gold
Serpents and seas and insects
The loosened universe flowing
Loathsome, limpid; there
Shines the eternal horror.

Gaiety and filth of birth!
Bodies grip, eyes' angles
Intersect the multiplicate netting
Of lives distinct and wrangling,
Each knot all others potential,
Friction, spark seminal
Of elders and outlanders.

Mirrors flashing each other:
That's the only proof
Let there be no absence!
The only solution,
Flash between mirrors
Not one, but many, but many!
Reason enough to go on with
And to bind my guides internal
To comb the suspect splendours
Love enough is enough
Presence craving
To speak in my action.

Frightened antinomies!
I have wiped example from mirrors
I have brought to heel my shadow —
Soul from her rebel heavens
My mirror's face and I
Are like no god and me
My death is my life's plumed gnomon,
Is a bride's embrace cruciform.
Reckless antinomies!
Asymptotes that gasp
Out of your element,
You shrink in the sunny mind
Now this fit is on me
And sealed mouths ripping
Tinctured with immediate
Usage which will agree to
No leave of absence
Let out their spate of birds

O fillers in of gaps!
Pure winged linking

To that which reflects me,
The third from the twain distinct not!
Is love of me in action.

His cliffs of ice are melted
Lord, thy wind with pollen!
Green land, be lilied with springs!
Where now my enemies? Gadflies
Dispersed. Favouring wind,
In your muttering silk fans
Winnowing the sundust, bring him!
Lord of delight and absence!
Thy bastions of light are taken
And our eyes like jewelled, subtle
Fish in thee are native
Lord of light shattered
Gathered now in my breast
Lord consubstantial
My pelican brood, my pleasure!

And sky is of his breath
With what tender pressure
He breathes his sky!

Tears from the depths, tears.
Desire glints in the peaks.
Groups of men and women!
Let existence lie female
To our crystal showers, his mirrors
Till, heaven over earth, we shape it
Into his cognation

And he will move breathing
Through us wing-linked

Proleptic of what Eden

Quiet blown in air
Lightened as if we were

Handy Andy

Out of the thighs the bosthoon comes
Blotched and blind and learning fright
To teethe the tigerish, rosy gums,
Fingers to feed the manual sight.

Who died? It was another.
I cried bitter, cried sore
Then got my moorhen in the heather
And slept and cried no more.

Ballad of Mistress Death

"Oh, I've had ten men before you,"
Said my redhead Sally,
"Yes, and a hundred men before you,"
Said my new-found darling.
The sea's blue maw glittered
Like a fat, barbaric queen's
And her thighs were white and gold
Like wisp-rain in sunshine.

In the long hall with statues
We sat and were not lonely,
Her name all forgotten,
My darkhead, my darling
Said in a gentle voice:
"And you never will be jealous
Though many's the man's head
Has lain upon my pillow,
For you've found out my secret
And many's the man more will."

"Yes, I've found out your secret,"
Said I to my darling,
Walking the dark streets
Through leaf-shaken lamplight.
"I never will be jealous
Nor you numb or nag at me
I'll name you the world's most beauty
Yellowheaded Helen
And no lie be telling;
No woman will disprove it."

She held me like nightfall
Her breath came like knives
While the housing plains sank lower
With their cinder-grates of cities —
Oh, there will need no porters
When all those doors open!

ANK'HOR VAT

The antlered forests
Move down to the sea.
Here the dung-filled jungle pauses

Buddha has covered the walls of the great temple
With the vegetative speed of his imagery

Let us wait, hand in hand

No Western god or saint
Ever smiled with the lissom fury of this god
Who holds in doubt
The wooden stare of Apollo
Our Christian crown of thorns:

There is no mystery in the luminous lines
Of that high, animal face
The smile, sad, humouring and equal
Blesses without obliging
Loves without condescension;
The god, clear as spring-water
Sees through everything, while everything
Flows through him

A fling of flowers here
Whose names I do not know
Downy, scarlet gullets
Green legs yielding and closing

While, at my mental distance from passion,
The prolific divinity of the temple
Is a quiet lettering on vellum.

Let us lie down before him
His look will flow like oil over us.

ON MOUNT MUCKISH

This hill could stage the end-play of a move
Of tribes their lifelong by the sagas haunted,
The peak-led lightning dramatize the roof,
The cairn sum up whole tent-sleep peoples depending
Like us on stones to record the hard-won norm
Through which our race its vagrant passion manned.
Put out of pet now, grooved in cyclic harm,
The close of death is grave, we will not rant.

Faint in the hullabulloo the ghostly tribes
Shake in our fathers' handsome act of death.
Temple, town-hall fall with silent pipes.
All the love-legends of the abandoned earth,
When the intestate loins have spent their race,
Would come to mind with tears and forfeit voice.

Meditation at Avila

Magnificence, this terse-lit, star-quartz universe,
Woe, waste and magnificence, my soul!

Stand in the window. Fountain waters
Bloom on invisible stems. Soul, my dear friend,
Welcome as always;
Fibrous listener in the darks of mind
Till my confession
Articulate your silence,
Pallas Athene through my beating temples.
Seed, sap and fruit.

You shall see blue arches of emptiness marching into the
  horizon
Over the yellow and black, the intolerant
Excellency of the Castilian highlands
All rock. And the sky
At its looped height
No pick or rope would clamber me up those impalpable
  crags of air!
If I could not talk to you
Fear would oppress me.

The Moroccan traveller says good night on the marble
  staircase
That rises round the great hall too blank for ghosts.
Flames in the brazier crouch; the hound chitters;
The traveller's housewife
Like a wife too long shut away in a new suburb
Chatters: through her inept words, the epileptic
Sacrifice of black bulls; almond blossom, oranges,

Anxious cultures among the wide, bronze, mountainous
wastes,
The sigh-spent wavetops of sierras;
Dance, the shellfish eaten, dance, the stertorous heels,
Sensual asseveration of bare thigh:
I stored her joy in my breast against the future.
Good night, the husband stands savouring a well-turned
jealousy;
The wife
Goes to him, sleepy and reluctant.
Contempt falls like a shadow between us.

Look out at the opened sluices of starlight,
Processionless plains with no
Humid corn or trees suckling or spectacular poppies,
Scarce earth but rock
Harsh as the forehead of Iahveh.

Nothing between
Rock and sky.
Santa Teresa
Her choirs of leaf-faced monks
Quavering like plain chant
Chanting to God to down
The Devil, his works and pomps.
The blue, absolute blow
Of linear Castilian night
Cleaves earth and heaven,
God being star-froze heaven
And Devil, fluent earth.
O Santa, Santa Teresa,
Covetous, burning virgin!
Scorning to nourish body's
Farmlands with soul's

Modulating rains,
You lost your eyes' rich holdings
To rubble, snakes and swine
And like the sceptical miser
You lost the usufruct
Of heaven, this floral life,
Hoarding to hasten it over
Death's barren, coughing border.

II

With fruitful diminution of my light,
Like Eve accomplisht out of Adam's side,
Soul glides, a glow of flesh, from out its packing.
Much have you left me thus, only to clear me
When chattels and truck of life too much have cumbered,
You, at once the radiance and the kindling
Of dream and deed sown in my travelling.
What is your word for me?
I hear: it is the seed, the sap, the fruit
All flowering in a doomed and sunny moment
From summer to summer; and you bring me
Comfort, my viaticum, journey-food;

Even though the full savour
Is edged with mortality;
And though your saving presence
Is never a promise, comes without warning
Or, being most wanted, fails:
Yet, soul, my long foreboding of the bone
And my green fire fermenting under loam
During the building, eating and sleeping,
When there is no actual advertence,
Thinking, not thinking, thinking of you

In streets of wheaten sunlight,
In love's body,
In the look of an old, bleak man
Nearing death
His shut coffer of fear under his arm;
Or when I see in front of the sky a great, sunny angel
Leaning on his elbows over a mountain,
Well may you come,
My self, seed of my suffering, seed
Of my want,
Fallen by the wayside,
Fallen among thorns, seed
Of my faith, my hope and my love!

Do you remember how, one night,
Staring up at the Milky Way,
Simplified like a parish registry recording only life and
  death,
With an ink-dim memory leafing back the centuries,
I watched the innumerable, witless cortege of the dead
Floating mute and baffled, they had died
All their desires fresh on their hastening lips,
They had gone out the door of life between two calls;
And I thought of the sigh of birdsong, stop and woodwind
  of
Starlings all up and down the green mile in the Ramblas,
While the stars wrinkled like crab apples with humorous,
  blue eyes;

O dead! O dead deprived! whose grief, filling my heart,
Called out for any reason for your rapt,
But called in alien silence, sensitive to
The hale and have of my humanity:
There, as I looked, so all a pity moved me

Groaning, I turned away with clenched fists
And there were you again,
Toothless, bald and smiling.

Old Jacobin

The round-backed river
Like a sleek, white cow
Shivers with day arriving
In the light of innocence
The slag is washed away
I make my soul, am peaceful
As though I had never sinned;

Never lied to the people
Lying to themselves
As I flagged them on with promises
Like the lover loving less than the beloved
Looking in her gentle face
Comforting her with lies.

The sun was gone from my father's garden
The white bodies vanished from the stream
And gunmetal twilight steeled my madness;
And I wore the pandemonium of the heroes.
But the antique stuffs I wrapt my virtue in:
Porous they proved to the maleficent winds
When prison walls
Roared in my ears high and black like thunder
The time I signed away the men I loved.
Where were the hero-selves that my imperium
Summoned from the *Odes,* the Roman *Lives*
To walk with me on the lawns in my green time?

II

Were they our forebears, then, the great dead?

The ghosts of children without bread and milk
Thronged my threshold; their fathers
Wept without tears.
I shouted in the Assembly; the deputies
Blushed in the drama. They knew and I
The Goddess Reason's treasonable trance.

Scarlet fuchsias open their honey
In the linen-pure morning. Here no children haunt me —
O chiming, ventral river, if thou wert Lethe!
Men of pleasure say I have wronged them
Who wronged themselves; hatred in their eyes
Like poor, shining straw.
The new President will fatten the poor:
But my factions in the misty pubs
Will strike the benches in shame
For the right denial, the personal curse foregone.

Still to quiet the children's crying, how I would give
My one blood and heart! But that was done, Christ!
Nor did that Tree bear like a round apple
The all good here; nevertheless
As the water bears the light equably
And as I will have no shame before my father
I bear my life
Without regret or praise.

Bitter watercress
Long water widening to where
There is but water and light and air.

ANTEROOM: GENEVA

The General Secretary's feet whispered over the red carpet
And stopped, a demure pair, beside the demure
Cadet, poor but correct,
Devoted menial of well-mannered Power.
"A word with you." "Yes, your Excellency."
Excellency smiled. "Your silk shirt is nice, Scriptor.
But listen. Better not let these private letters
Reach the President. He gets worried, you know,
About the personal misfortunes of the people;
And really, the Minister is due to arrive.
It is surely most unseemly
To keep the State in the waiting-room
For God knows what beggars,
For totally unnecessary people."

Their mutual shirtfronts gleamed in a white smile
The electorate at breakfast approved of the war for peace
And the private detective idly deflowered a rose.

Argument with Justice

Virtue all men stand under, what wonder, blinded on thy
  column transcendental, thou art
Sterile, since not bedded with man thy secular wooer who
  could waken thy
Dreams to bloom; and why blinded?
Darest not take, not take to thy sight these anarchic, thy
Realms of thy reign abandoned?

Anchorite of the aether, thy influence in the brain quivers
  but tenuous . . . with what desperate antennae, dearest!
  and thy
Lamps in our breast fret out; no less does thy bruised
  forehead anger us like the
Great limed birds, Isaiah and Chartres in the
Pensioner hold of thy sisters, cold heraldic
Mercy and Charity sour-dugged.

Widowed of our seed which would leaven and make serial
  thee, marmoreal in the hangings of heaven, welcoming
Nature's moan as an ever imminent epithalamium, know
  that, hooded, thy
Dream of will's no will flowering in
Action, blowzed menstruate, wasting till some fancied
Excellence fit thy arrival.

Rigid, breathless to scare not thy death-heeled steps, O
  novice, we should wait thee, as pure and dawnlit, thy
Guardians, the elder cliffs of the first country to chant and
  entemple thee,
Born beside an unstrung blue
Sea and trembling its transparence in thy mien, O equable!
O crags and crushed-foam beauty!

Beautiful named because from time abstract and therefore
  sacrosanct? Ah, what good! if the
Cunning have bandaged thee thus with eternity, turned
  thee lodestar blandishing them and the
Innocent in the ignorant ruin of
Kingdoms and fevered republics babbling dry-lipped
Beneath thy blind silence?

Blown, see, against thy portals, centuries of mortals mouth
  blasphemy righteous: "What reward for
Fasting, and why, the future clasped, must the present ring
  of diverse winds puff out in
Vanity? She will not come down
Lest our contentment then should prove her jealous
Heaven untrue." Virtue

Virtue of all men, fear not that we thy temple crumble, flesh
  crumbles, but
Not till the mind's raped out. Fear rather thy name be
  forgotten from father to
Son, or by thy saints. Come down, let there be
Justice though the heavens fall, be virtue of our
Temporary measure.

Pays Conquis

The invader came again and conquered
With the old by-product crimes
But three years later the harvest flaunted,
The young kept faith with Time.
The invader built bridges, roads
Feeding the pastures to the ports;
Endowed schools where experts learned
To drain the steam rebellion churned.
The mayor, the general forgot
Jean and Jacques unjustly shot.

And when the careless earth brought forth
Well-fed children, wheat and coal
More than the laws provided for:
The shadowy experts muffed their role;
Jacques in his widow's bed was hate,
The rifles hid by Jean were bared
To win back pride in free estate;
And refuse paper flew in the square
Outside the scared Proconsulate.

Boy Bathing

On the edge of the springboard
A boy poses, columned light
Poised.
Seagulls crying wrinkles
The brown parchment cliffs.
His body shines: a knife!
Spread wings, he opens
Plunges
Through the gold glass of sunshine
Smashes
In crumbs of glass the silence.

Bacchanal

Forerunners, with knees flashing like scissors, raced by the hostile telegraph wires,
Start for the ships with the news, Cut Through, all is against them despair inspires:
The poor made limp by want and cackling, brainstopped youth, a seaweed crowd . . .
How the road that smokes through the mountains, whose panther-bounding shadows applaud, is loud
With the confident feet of pursuing criers! their eyes diamond with thousands of years
Of domination and lands held of fictitious papers by right of fears,
Easy on which to maintain the sneering feet of the lovely lords of might,
They and the courtiers of prudence insured against danger of life and number and light.

Forerunners run naked as sharks through water, nose to their prey, have message by heart,
Their thighs will be tackled, Look Out, They're Away! clipping the wind, they've gained on their start.
The wind thrusts knives in their teeth, harrows the stubble of parched throats,
The front line licks its fire, leaderless, can they cut their way to the boats?
They have never eaten or drunk or slept their fill, and have no quick-wit means,
Only envy learnt in feeding the shutfist, pistoned, right machines.
Canaille, canaille, what red horizons of anger for humbled lives lie

Tumbled up in the old times, the long-fermenting now, canaille!
Tradition, if wanted, you can taunt with bequeathed pain, unslaked hate,
For neither the slow-travelling signal from the pyramid builders comes too late,
In spite of imposed ignorance, No, nor intelligence from a brave new State.

Death, starvation among the corn and coal stored in bankrupt winter,
Bent-rail backs of daily slaves and soiled skin under accosting banter
Of flashbabies in back-quarters: where meetings froth loud to a rebel note.
Useless. For after smokescreen luxury penitent, cocky plebeians trot;
And putrescent tenements breed vermin, tearing holes in occasional rags,
Fume from sour mouths of windows, whimper on senile, quicksand legs.
Raucous the air and barb-tongued, seasoned with tunes from slit-eyed bars,
Where, living on credit in blabbing pints, the anger of cities boozy stares:
G.P.I., poxed brows: *"Oh, what the hell! All the duties and damn all rights!*
They can't get away with it, they shall pay for it, up to the neck in it, blast the skites!"

How shall we suffer the little children to come unto us, how shall we pay
For the ranged, amorphous faces grey as the creased skies this guttering day?

While pushbelly, hunger-currency laymen, cultivating the
liquorice flowers
Of their happy entrails, hand in hand, dance around earth-
produce pyres
And religious scarecrows navigate with downcast eyes this
vale of tears?

Already immense shoulders heave edgeways through heavy
bales of sleep.
Force of confederate, free flangewheels, O runners through
breakage! give them the slip:
Those with hands like shrinking linen that deprecate the
state of affairs,
Parsing attitudes, fleas in intricate corridors of interlocking
hairs,
Those that are Not So Sure that the Poor in Pogrom will not
be Rather a Bore,
Lips bitter-sweet, they Know by Culture, they know Human
Nature can Grow no More;
Those that are Game to Grin and Bear it, those that the
Wear and Tear of, that hesitate
Wagging advice faded and steaming as old maids' clothes
before the grate,
Those that My Country, that Let Us Pray, that Drop by the
Way, those that are Late . . .
Oh, when damned by the sentence of guns advancing like
ants in tragic line
And stowed away in Death, their own hungry mirror, it will
be fine!

The blood beats drums in the runners' temples, the news is
safe as yacht in cove.
And hearts, throbbing squadrons of nocturnal seaplanes,
moving stars above

Stars fixed in the sea, it will be fine, the ground is cleared,
  material stored,
With fervid violence, come, forerunners, release the news at
  this anxious port.
Red trains lap up the licking rails, east the horizon snarls
  alarms:
Relief from the wheatfields, printing presses toss their
  tresses with steel arms.
Come up! Up up! The thunder at one with your voices in
  order chants, things
Are with you, rolling her rump, Earth in bacchantic rumbas
  grave swings,
Multiple antennae of blind gunnery tremble, invest the
  fibrous night
And the armies' crystal shock makes laughter of girls in a
  forest pool out of sight.

Is it true, is it true, have you seen the syllables travel over
  lips, have you seen
Beermugs whirled through battered lyrics, children ring
  embrace on the green?
Bright women thrown in laughter, Oh gay, Oh nothing
  need anything refuse,
Goldstocking legs in their white foam swinging, a country
  singing joy of the news?

Joy Joy an unbetweened chorus crowds the air with sound
Burgeoning, they feel surging more loud the birth of well-
  being all around
While curvetting aeroplanes, leaflets released, toss through
  the matador swords of the sun
And the ships cheered by the seminal hail of the captain, by
  the people won,

Draw white clothes on, make sure of the sea, open tanned arms with love and take
To the long white heather of the waves, a wind of towns in cry in wake.

Forerunners with eyes of dangerous landscapes silent among the cheering sigh
At the flocks of aeroplanes grazing at stall across the spring prairies of the sky.

After Five o'Clock

A government official dressed in grey minor
Slipped into a low pub
At the end of the world;
Outside, the rain was falling in millions.

An ancient like a frittered, chalk hill
Monocled the evening paper through a chip of
  window-pane:
The disgraced words took on dignity.

''Will he tout me for a drink?'' feared the Government
  official
Though the ancient stirred no more than a thought in a
  new-dead man.

ANNAPOLIS

"No, we can't get a licence for liquor, being too near the church,"
Said the waiter. The church looked friends enough
On its humble, grassy hillock. So I said: "Excuse me,
I must have a drink." And I rambled on down West Street
To eat and drink at Socrates the Greek's.
On my right at the Raw Bar, a truckdriver drinking milk
And a Norwegian second mate glared at their faces
In the mirror. We floated on heat
Like paper boats boys prod in the bathroom.

The white-linen cadets walked with girls of good family
It was the feast-day of the Republic and the girls
In long dresses made a drawing room of the streets;
They were like sweet william and buttercups
Like petunia and sweet pea and silver moss,
The *haute couture* clapped a little askew
On their melodious immaturity.
As I said to the truckdriver: "They are children."
He flashed a sigh and said: "Indeed they are."

Imperceptibly darkness plucked its petals
You hear the coloured people's viola laughter
And starlight one never looks up to
Blurs the woollen trees
And the houses with no comment to make. A delicate drunk
Weaves his glass limbs together up the street.

The little, red-brick capital,
Its velvet, burgess elms,

Curls back into childhood
Trumpets and tricorns, arteries of fern.
I hold my breath for the expected
According to the mechanics of fairyland.

But then, it is not Hans Andersen, the monuments
Of power lour as in any London. Cadets conduct
Camera-fans to the Governor's residence
To the Capitol and the Revolutionary General
Leading ghosts on his enthusiastic stone horse.

In the porches, after dinner
Loud-bellied citizens swat flies.
The band blows open the Academy gates
And there a girl-dancer remotely
Flows to the dance.

Tantalus

The diplomat has bared his head,
The wine spreads across the cloth.
Give me stones for leavened bread?
My spine's pipette will fume in wrath.

I knew a gifted girl, she spoke
Languages more than Noah's beasts
She took the veil and loathed the yoke,
Flirting despair with Mormon priests.

What will you give me if I tell?
I cannot speak, my hands are tied
Shame like an Alderman in Hell
Has broke me down till I have cried.

The Blind Leading the Blind

Half-hearted, hum low, hide from my
Fool, that my familiar is,
Pride slipt on shabby genteel shoe.
Hide the fear and check the spleen.
Lightning like a fever chart
Quickens the last, quick stare at life;
Storm destroys but cunning can
Find crevice there; speak to him, say:
"Be my obedience for a spell
The fugitive causeway fingers sight
Hold your breath like hunting moon
I'll feint with the steering wheel, come through."

Storm hunts the moon through heathery skies
The moon at bay reveals her cover
Light up the windscreen, clears the way
For causeway's clouts of wind and dark;
And my fool fawns on me
His cheek on mine, takes the wheel,
Muzzles my mathematics, his
Nails deaden my temples, breath
And gibber mixed beside my eyes.
Fear melts in the storm, danger
Grows in me till I exult,
Wave the arm, sing and defy
The strapped, consumptive seas beneath.

Every step the first and last
Curlews along their stretch of coast
Rattle their figurative bewares,
Guardian fowl but capped like us,

Cry our number, cry our want!
Hear the measure in my voice.
Sky opens and would take us
With its thirsty light; and we
Proceed above the hooked rocks.

Freedom No Object

Here are empty quaysides
It might be midnight nearby
Or a searchlight stripe on midnight.

Enter, stealthy, who-you-know
Propelled along in torpor
He might be a river flowing
Back to the source, its author

He is pulled up short
By stacks of sacked grain. He
Pushes, his legs move
Up and down and free.

Celibate Recusant

In the jingling, clear air,
Skim over the Temple domes
Birds, those fishes with hair.

Remember the signa fish were
In the incoherent catacombs,
Wombs that gave but mixed birth.

In a tunic, striped and cool,
I lie on the red earth,
Over me kneels my Fool.

Floats from a far shrine
A Virgin, pure of male girth.
The upper air seethes to brine.

She is the first unlike All Them,
Jerusalem! Jerusalem!

She planes down over me,
Endymion and the Moon I see.

"Unclean! Unclean!" my Fool cries,
Hatred of me frees his eyes.

I jerk out what comes next
In the ritual of slaves of slime,
My fear all unstrung:

"Touch me not!" to the unsexed,
Abstract, furious Virgin hung

Above me, time after time

And like a great, dull fish
She floats on: "It's as you wish."

Obstacle Basilisk

Down the path through treacherous years blood-dried
My cold-sweat horse, with his incredulous ears,
Ticks off each bandit landmark as we ride,
With friendly snuffling shows he shares my fears.
Those damp rhinoceroses, the mountains, shamble
Past; and hasty clouds tear like bramble
Into its spectral seven the dying light;
The stirrup foot, the reins, renegue their lordships,
A mile below is a breastful of warships
In a heroic harbour, menacing, tight.

An old priest's nag pulls up, cries askance
At our disarticulated style:
"Halleluia! halleluia!" In fractious dance
His legs curve like a weak smile.

Then sundown at the city gates
Defended by a groom and three sick colts
My horse backs away and defecates,
Transformed into a whippet, off he bolts:
I have lived with nobility of emotion,
Thought out my honour, justified my rise:
Is this mean groom my measure? he, my harm?
Shall thus his fear degrade me, slow my arm?
The basilisk, my mercy in his eyes,
Unmans us both; we fade in slow motion
By invisible spider-camera webbed; our cue,
Predestined, robs us of the will to do.

Or could I ever break the servile charm
And gain one step, in scrupulous alarm?

DAPHNE STILLORGAN

The stationmaster is garrulous in
The modest station set in the glen
Bushes wink with brown birdwings
The benches spread their knees, present
Drowsy laps to the sun.
A white cat sacred dangerous within
Egyptian memories considers
Like a marksman a celluloid ball on a water-jet
A tigermoth's fatal rise and fall
On her rank breath.

One shadow makes the whole sky shake
But I flick with instantaneous eyes
The next quick change before the change begins.
The water spouts are dried
Laurel leaves
Shine in the waxen summer.

The clean metronome of horses' feet on the road
Made anguish with clocks and rules which now
Silence beyond measure floods again
Through the trees' green bazaar and patches
Of light like muslin girls in forest lost.
And lost, but after noisy pebble wrinkling
This scene became a pool in air limpid
Restoring to the inimitable Images
Reflections paled but smooth as smooth as smooth.

Fuchsias revive and breathe through scarlet mouths
Rumours on wind
Far-off the humid pounding of a train

Wind-cylinders boom along
Steel wires, the rails drone,
Far-off thudding, trampling, thud
Of thousand pink-soled apes, no humorous family god!
Southward, storm
Smashes the flimsy sky.

Vines, virgins, guard your red wine
Cross branching arms frail on breasts
Small showers will fall before the rain crowds:
Use them to cool your rind-stiffening flesh
Writhing with blood for sap
To suck the insect-pointed air, the first threat
Of eager ravishers.

Scared faces lifted up
Is the menace bestial or a brusque pleiad
Of gods of fire vagabond?
Quick just in time quick just in time; ah!
Trees in light dryad dresses

Birds (O unreal whitewashed station!)
Compose no more that invisible architecture.

Welcome My World

My white tiger bounding in the west!
Only eternal, animal and dumb,
  Give me my merited rest.
The end of Time is when my time is come.

My two arc-lamp globes muttering light
My thorax of wild woodbine offered
  Staid, fiery and slight.
My dark room where voiceless chairs are proferred.

My green dragon from the barbarous east!
Bring the light with ropes of shaken rain
  April swells in yeast,
A baffled virgin with a knocking brain;

The flesh bound in flat, rasping scales,
Reptile, to your fugacity I cling.
  My witch of nursery tales,
My everything, my thou, my everything!

Gannets casually stab the sea.
Each hunting wave envies the next its pleasure,
  Surround me
The spine is blank, body is pure measure.

Marble protectress with vigilant breasts,
His enemy armed against the curious sun,
  Safe in the dark, the chests
May be opened and your treasure won.

My black tortoise from the hatching north!
Geysers and hissing streams, the landlocked sea
    Are back and forth
Beneath the snail and the sleeper with crooked knee.

My olive naiad in Ionian creeks,
My ballad maiden raped in Highland forays,
    World all in fable speaks,
My gun-flanked heroine of detective stories.

Rise and look out the window and dress,
Mother with child, old man with mottled laughter,
    World, be my guest!
And sleep again, go to sleep after

My feast: I'm blind! if oiled athletes preen
Their animal in the glass, if priests refute
    Seen with divine unseen,
I'm dumb, my world, without your light, I'm mute.

Return my early my Lisbon rapture, the galleons
Glittered in from Goa rich and mean,
    Immoderate like stallions,
And the sky in chevalier plume-doff of green

And scarlet kept the burghers in suspense:
Glitter and flit, let others envy me,
    Starling, starlet, what pretence
Could any mortal make to let you be?

Dancing with you is dancing with
Water, ashes kindle on my mouth
    To inform you with,
O my red phoenix from the south!

SUMMER JUJUBE

"Give a tip to the chimpanzee on the hanging-bridge."
Bodiless voices will get no change out of me!
The chimpanzee in commissionaire dress
Accepts my Scots coin with disdainful grace.

Dried cliffs hold the blue cove
With brown market-woman arms around
Baskets of fruit. High the cliffs hum
Pinged with voices which a metal bird
Pecks and drops in flat echoes over
Hives in clefts and bee-serviced furze.

And tracing on emphatic, limited scale
Their needle notes, the self-deluded larks
Keep a faint, fixed idea cork-bobbing
In the wanton, berry heads of convent girls
Fretful on the apathetic sand;

Among them one, a bold, a billboard baggage
Like a primping principal boy at the pantomine
Keeps the far-galleried chimp on dancing hoof.
She fires her thighs with hands to learn their office,
Patting her pleasure in her mockeried men.

The Easter vestments of the heat crackle
And egg-backed ladybird and bluebottle,
He of the glossy, royal-blue rump,
Rub sleepy legs without looking.

Now dips her runaway horse, a white sail
Over and down waves of stone ditch,

Rears in invisible lariat, scared
By briary winter sly beneath the bloom.

Her whip exclaims. Horse, to your world return;
Mistress is landmark; friend, the hound
Pouring like milk into his sleep.

Damson on the springboard,
She smiles for the fun of it through orange lips,
Divides the air, the idle water.

Poet and Comic Muse

Actress, head tilted, hithering smile,
Advance, advance against me,
Twittering proliferation pruned to style.
Sterilized in us, their passions stare,
Incontrovertible in the floodlit glare.
Come, bunted out in borrowed quips;
You have both enjoyed and incensed me,
We are suspended on the line between our lips.

I am glad no disobedience can
Disarray this axiomatic plan:
The rite
Unrolls with the casual necessity of a bullfight;
Pinned on the euclidean frame
On the stage, night after night,
Always our sentence and remand the same.

Laugh with your mouth.
On fiction fixed, the general, vague drouth
Is slaked by the neat passion we do:
And winning them I can approach you.

Victory of Samothrace

Hammers musical round my head, hammers throbbing on
the roofs
Wary silence of brutal propellers that have suddenly burst
their speed
All aboard all calling all in all in!
Smell in the rain of mown hay and thistles, old
Red of poppies, creeping warmth of remembered desire.
Heads are markets for anarchic holdings
Are there no shoulders to lean on?
A sweet lady! not alas the invented Lady of Serenity

Fingers of a black-gloved hand tender and vicious on my
throat
I am snatched up and hurled into the air
Sweet lady! on this grey sea you are not preceded by
singing dolphins, as was Aphrodite
But by discord of winds
Nor by the noise of drums, drums throbbing continuous
hammers
But are yourself the creator of tornado with your clothes
whirring about your knees like grouse rising
And your wings
Disturbing the exact harmony of the stars

Victory, winged Victory!

The sea is empty of fish beneath me and there are no ships
Otherwise I should cry for help
But making the best of my own bargain
I offer you as gauges of faith
The beginnings all over again

The never to be forgotten and
The supposed brightness of lamps in daytime

Winged Victory of Samothrace!

Let me be always in this state of grace
Keep me going on bribes like this, the unfinished
  handiwork of sunset
Be to me also for a sign
Of burgled outhouses round the inviolable family stone
As a priest uncertain among his mysteries when a bending
  candle flame provokes forbidden images.

A man is swung between two lilies tall as pines. Terror!
Increasing loudness of a thousand feet of men tramping
  down wooden stairs. Throbbing wooden stairs.
I will make another prayer
Give me an object of art, a statuette of Diana
I will caress her limbs closely with my fingers

For these graces, spirit of movement, I will build you an
  altar
To be destroyed immediately
And make offerings of promise
Of heroes once again
Of women's eyes before love has drowned their sweetness.
The moment is poised in fear

Our Lady of Victory!

And your voice, which has the opulent contentment of a
  June stream, babbles
And I feel with relief:
Better in danger with the goddess than float like a barge on

the sea:
Fingers again at my throat

Baptism by immersion in the numerous sea

As the water closes over me, I see
The impersonal gleam in your eyes
And the lax ebb and flow of your breasts.

THE LANCET

Brilliant fierce eagles
And goldfishes asleep.

Lips to drink and instruments for singing
Tight hedgerows gripped the fields, now loose and
  drowsed.
I moved about in the dark, all was quiet
The skies swollen with unshed thunder
Along the clay path my footsteps
Ominously, softly counted time.

Everyside are spread the fruitful plains
Villages live and die
Beneath the million-citied sap, the indifferent fosterage
Of trees; bloom of night!
As the bloom of black grapes to your nocturnal sky:
So am I near to freedom.

Now and then a shout floats up
In the court
Where the colleagues
Are drinking and musing. None
Will propose an enigma.

Look straight into my eyes when you drink: Yes;
The same enchantment as ever makes me yours!

Your hair dims
I narrow my eyes to slits and I see
Gold copes gliding
The market places foaming with white smocks

Cantilenas of men and women chained and chanting
Each mouth fabulous
With its proper version.

I have been held back
From acts of particular kindness;
I have skulked in the halls of anger
And with meanness have blighted
The blossom of generous givers

But make it that I tremble
In Babylon choirs, in sonorous congregation
The celebration of belled buildings
And turn by turn stare without terror on
The rapt ravelling and unravelling of tidal generations
In which I am born and give birth and die;
And above that sea
Simple and full the sun.

The drinkers topple over
Come, we are still asleep.
Avoid the lunar marshes

Darkness slips
From my face, your voice
Clamours in my blood
The same enchantment as ever!
Your drowsy head,
Dishevelled, falls on my shoulder.
The streams in their beds
Never tire of habit
The same enchantment!
Ebony doors open, my love
Is unfulfilled, yield!

The brothers of the sun, the eagles,
Are fixed among the wavering skies, yield!
Bear fruit of me.

Venus of the Salty Shell

Round a cleft in the cliffs to come upon
The Athenians standing with their friendly gods
Serious on the shore.

The fresh violet of the Middle Sea
Blooms and is gone; and there
The tremble of a difference from the foam
Foam forms a shell which bears
The smiling idol of Love
Brightness shadowy through brightness.

The space of a moment love lightens the body
Only when love comes free as air
Like the goddess on the dove-drawn shell
Riding upon the speckled hawthorn waves
Into the rocky ways of the sea-republic.
Look at that hand gently to the breast!
She smiles as if turning all the orchards of summer
Into one brittle petal to touch.

The old men do not remember
The women of their youth,
The young men bend at point like setters.
There is need; she, the desired-with-cries,
Fanned by the ivory air, on the ache of birth
Advances as though her nakedness
Were the first glad woman's for these men

And nearer and the cries of the men
Stop, they are struck still.
The doves, the hawthorn merge in the wrack and foam.

Edinburgh Tale

I love walking with you in the Prince's Street all twinkling
with strangers' eyes,
The telephone chirrup, the downandouts fit in.
I love your eyelids, leaves landing; armistice settling down
Over a whole wired, limb-laundering province where a
yellow-hammer
Singing, brings on weak tears;
There is a song from Sean's country
A death aside in the slums,
Your eyes lit up like a theatre.

In the marshland, in moonlight, a hunter drags home.

I love your hands of a drowning man gripping a spar; your
arms flung wide
Like the forgiving rainbow, and what has been done is
Vain, vain, I love your hands

The shouldered earth
By force lit up and darkened
The rivers through earth's breast

Rose of crystal

And your voice and when you listen:
Arras of the Queen's room in Holyrood
The lute is crisp, the bible voices fervid with scandal,
The lute's notes fall like seeds on the straight, yellow petals
of your feet.
Rose of June, said the peasants in their ballads
Rose of June!

That Queen, fair body stemmed in cramoisy

Ballads of the donjons jerked up in the brown Lowlands,
Whose mistresses so fine, so rare-ringed,
Secret inside three walls
Kin-blood, their robes of cramoisy:
Alack, had love no luck, old gossip, and lust kill?

The tale ends for having been
No secret after all but the ungovernable, scared birds of the heart and the blood risen and the lute like an idiot
I unleash my footpads on your heart
Your heart saying the same word over and over again to itself like a happy child.

Between the Late and Early

A drink for a drouth!
What summer have you dried in me,
Holding for taste your body rare?
Give as your mouth
Does, liberal kisses open there
Of all shades like the anemone.

It will be all one
When we tire; but now, ageing suspended,
Loving can stroke day into night.
What have you done
Sweet to my gall? Love, starting light,
Like travel reversed, heavy must end it.

Brighten and be
An amber ounce of June's breath.
Love's favourites are few
Let him have me
And you all instant you all of you!
Nothing will need us after death.

Eve in My Legend

The world turns round and leaves the sun.
City fathers, light her way!
Switch on the lights for her! It's done,
For her the town's a Milky Way.
I am near mindless, I could mime
The passions that consume Time.

Today we passed from a yellow street
Into a black one, high and cold
I said to her, I turned it neat,
"Your hair's the sun now, warmth and gold."
The too few suns whose earth, to thrive
Can but in Love's eyes come alive.

Once I had kissed her eyes and seen
My love there made whole by their rays
I knew her better than if we'd been
Together a hundred nights and days
And air whose sunny tongues are birds
Bore with ease our heavy words

As she from my drugged side took life.
I feel like Adam who in sleep
Gave birth to Eve, daughter and wife
Whence his far brood would sow and reap,
Half monster, half philosopher,
Movement by mood conceiving her.

And now stop for a mental spell
The forest-eyed, obsidian After!
Yet let that hundred-headed tell

My arms full of her blond laughter
Nothing to know that is not she
Nor she know anything but me.

Wishes for Her

Against Minoan sunlight
Slight-boned head,
Buildings with the thin climb of larks
Trilling off whetstone brilliants,
Slight head, nor petal nor marble
Night-shell
Two, one and separate.

Love in loving, all
A fledgeling, hard-billed April,
Soil's gaudy chemistry in fission and fuse.
And she
Lit out of fire and glass
Lightning
The blue flowers of vacant thunder.

In the riverlands
Stained with old battlefields, old armour
In which their child, rust, sighs,
Strangers lost in the courtyard,
I lie awake.
The ice recedes, on black silk
Rocks the seals sway their heads.

No prophet deaths
In the webbed tensions of memory,
No harm
Night lean with hunters.
I wish you well, wish
Tall angels whose rib-freezing
Beauty attend you.

Little Elegy

I will walk with a lover of wisdom
A smile for Senator Destiny
But I shall gladly listen.

Her beauty was like silence in a cup of water
Decanting all but the dream matter.
The figures of reality
Stood about, Dantesque and pitiful.
Can anyone tell me her name?
I will love her again and again
Girl on skis, arrow and bow in one,
Masked in glass, graceful,
Hard as a word in season.

I saw a round, Bavarian goodman
And a Harvard student with a Mohican's lope
Colliding with huge nosegays
Then laughter burst above their flowers:
Absent of mind, they had their wits about them
I laughed at them both outright

And at simpering, peasant statues
Graces and gods would they be!
It was a heady springtime in Munich
Many I knew confided in me
Popu, the champion cyclist
Sigmund, deriding tyrants
And Carlos, who made love shyly
To a furtive, gentle girl
And came to my door, stammering,
''She loves me, you know.''

"She loves me, you know."

But geography separated them
And geography keeps them apart
Now they live forgotten in each other's heart.

II

The sun was full on, the bird-breed
Gradually found their wings.
The baroque churches glowed like the Book of Kells.
We two, with butterbrot and sweetmilk
Over the snow beneath blue winds
Went far and wide.
Busy, alone, we all go far and wide
Who once listened to each other's
Fair vows and counsel.

Of those that go out of the cafés and the gardens
Some lie in prisons
Some die of unhappiness
Indeed, it is so!

This is all I can remember
Quarrelling, gusts of confidence
The class climbing through faun nights
And her I would meet
As though I were unconscious
In vacant, bright-columned streets
And beings in love's tunic scattered to the four winds
For no reason at all
For no reason that I can tell.

Picture in a Window

"Les roses sont tantôt passées et les rossignols aussi."

— RACINE

Roses are past and nightingales as well.
The mercury streams, this mouse-leaf-moving dell,
Old, rusty yards beneath autumnal rain.
Here, in the climate of grief, deciduous bane
Of the faithful heart, the humbled Hercules
Puzzles illiterate accident's decrees;
Here, tired of interlacing, naiads crave
The novel-boned boy and lascivious wave
Moist thighs and hips and stare with mucous eyes,
Untended now their river sources rise.
Your finished, angular health their sense enthralls;
Descend, Elysium behind the falls
Grows love-in-idleness, descend, Hylas,
Form the damp impulse of that female mass.

II

Webs of wet gaslight thread the streets and lanes,
In pavement runnels and in spiderous drains
Oily putrescence clots in painted dams
Which, as my memory, her double, shams
Its blacked-out crystal springs, are flaked with rain
Like scruples in the circumambient brain.
And Hercules fills the offended coffee-stands
With rippling echolalia, his hands
Around wine-cups remember slender hips,
The beechleaves touch his face with waning lips.

The buildings through their thousand windows burn
Saffron in the fog and heads to lilies turn:
O buildings! Wrestling, incandescent tree!
Fewer you burn than want of her in me,
As her smile, leaf-orphan of the streets,
Beckons from mouth to cheating mouth, retreats.

III

No more the inspired hoarding of the fire
In time which most you hate and most desire
(Unless, as sages say, each minute thing,
This beetle and this beetle's broken wing,
Discard their sensual harnessing to rise
A Beatific Buzz in Azure Skies!)
Ah, how, like buds clouded with dew, the skin
Shrank from and craved the listening fingers in
As different loves unite with what they miss!
White moon, white moon, O grant us, Artemis,
Thy gift of lunacy lest bleed afresh
The wound of separation of the flesh;
Lest I relive, mature in swaddling clothes,
That trauma between racket and repose,
Or see in the dark her corndusky hair,
The breath held in, the foot upon the stair.

FAREWELL AND GOOD

She I loved so much will not appear again
Brilliant to my eyes as once she held me, nor
To inhuman eyes in any angel-foaming world.

What use my hermit grief to a world bitten in self,
Bland under omen, but to make more its useless griefs?
Why must, as absence ages, she the more instant cling?

Grief cannot doctor my birthday evil that diminished her
Nor be voucher for recompense of pain at heaven's gates
Nor by crying it for relief do I purge it. Nothing forgets:

Not wisdom teased from the wax and crumble of all flesh,
Powdering between thumb and finger: O wash in
  moon-milk!
Suck the drug simples in our rock-night scratched by man

In eruptions of mineral continents scuffling to settle down:
Nor though spring lust and shine on the sea and chaffinches
  chatter,
Though light from sunlight down to tombs give me my
  kind:

Whatever I do, unreal, I may find my hand, once hers,
Bled on the wall in a crack of anger and veins blocked
And eyes glazed that will break open to hers no more;

At any time of the day and night, struck by a wind-flash
In snood of leaves or in phantasms of sleep assembling her
  form,
I restore my kingdom in her, the real that deepened the
  dreamed-on

Ritual loves of legend women admired in childhood:
Then remembrance stings my reason, both entangled in
Grief which webs movement and is merely want.

Still the complaint, still no comfort to her and me split
Like a glass, like life spilt by some Sistine hand,
Our life that brimmed over like diamonds in our light.

Love from Time To Time

It is the drained head
The mustang tilt of the chin
Farewells hardly count

The passion that was a third life
And we its yolk and white
Has cracked its shell. Can we feed alone?
For the first time I see you clear.
Where is the source of tears?

Day turns over and it is night.
Patient beds, neither wanting nor wanted.
The pouting breasts, the intake of the lap
What are you, dried for want of our sleep?
Let be the thirst, I cannot slake it
The underswell of Time whispers me away.

II

What coasts are these we cling to but the world's
Its walls raised by the frail, learned sight
Which, as they noise down in disaster,
Beguile my ears to thin out the tinkling
Of their most precious panes, wealth and art,
Where are you and I
In the brass flames of our mistress city on fire?

Now courage at love's ending cowers before
Love's transmissions censored in your eyes.
May the whipcord train
Snap and let out from my station! Yet,

O shoulders bent filial
Face in depthless vulcanite washed
From neither's past, from the underlip of the world,
Who smile away, now in another mood,
Self-pity and the fear of hardship
Who make love all and neither here nor there:
Still, still, the wound lives beneath the breast.

III

It's the last barricade, the defenders of the capital kill with spades.
Absence is only winter, the valley
Shouldering Nile will flood.
The pointed, clean linen and stiff glass are ready.
After months of familiar darkness
That glinting scarab, the sky, renews the heliacal
Rising of Sirius, daylight
Which does not believe in death.

Lo! lo! that red, absent drumming!
I have your fingers tight held;
In a few days, the lapse apart
Of our bodies, they, our motor and term.

Nearer than hands as we were
My eyes' membrane went silk with childhood;
Imagine then however one we were
In swift, carnival streets with sanguine flags,
Now your eyes are inert, you are faced away:
Sweet or bitter farewells, it's all a matter.

Love made, there is nothing to thirst for.
Love cymbals the interior hour, the dancer
Fretted out from its blood.

A Dream of Orpheus

Low and knelt on my heels at the blank bed in moonlight
Listening with sidelong frightened eye to the forms of the
  table
Twitching out of inanimate wood, all form erratic,
Night-risen mineral and plant loose from man's neat
  dominion,
I stroke and stroke the sheets murmuring the old
  endearments:
''Little mouth of honey! thyme breath! lamp of my
  comfort!''
(O Love! sweet protestant soul of pain and guilt and death!
Better be crost and leave like an ignorant avid youngster
Whose gay-plumed brain in dreams dances his body's
  need.)
But here's a ghost's hand only I hold; and heartsick I think
  of
Your eyes' Cyprian charm from sacred, ivory centuries,
We lying, balanced in night's blue hammock in bright upset
And earnest lark singing so brilliant to faint-come sun
I willed them both in my arms; nor I but the lark called him
Lord of the world, lord! nor I moved, but earth, from sleep.

Now, again, the hour between night and morning softly
Holds city, rock and beast companion in nets of wisp;
Orpheus I am not whose grief sang so melodious, the lion
Shyly drew back his ears, yawned and the sycamore
  drooped its
Branches as now they are; who, powered by magic,
  descended
Deeper than the pits of guilt to Hell's void, and singing
Conquered back his Eurydice murdered, and Death warned

him:
"Turn from her yet the terror of human eyes, for death is
Only life's limpness, or she will lapse back with the
shades."

Lost Eurydice! beautiful through chance of change on
change . . .
Life, whose indifferent labouring only love can bear with,
Bared to gold-nerved rock: and there rises a pastoral world:
Farmers, serfs of the rain, shrunken wives, goat-smells,
The hunchback wheat to cut, the hunter and his hunger,
Lifelong enemies in that boat blandly sailing to death
(Master from anywhere, comfort them!) all lie, remotely
harmonious,
In the god's lazy eyes. But in the halt of evening, murder!

Bareness of stone is stone listening, fear and trembling
Take doe pausing with doubled paw, pigeon on half-wing,
And men seeing the forms they knew denatured. Then
Orpheus,
Priest with power over words, called, so unselfed by pity
that
Generosity gave him power over things, called her name:
She with kind hands had wedged the waste in the eternal:
Humbly the hills drew near with shadowy, compassionate
arms
And as though the dead had suddenly wakened and asked
for silence,
Silence was; and he murmured, chanted his grief till the
beasts,
Nozzle sloped on paw, dimly adored her name and
Lilt-foot fawns nudged bravely up to the quiet wolf-packs
Terrified as all the articulated world trembled apart
At murder's torpid sacrilege: till Orpheus, finder in frenzy,

Sang out the mortal sympathy linking plant, beast and man.

Rise, turn away. And come, O fresh and slim-wind
  morning!
Love's summer-syllabled arbor ripens to silent autumn.
Rock lessens; creatures grow and fail; the hunter
Ages in the ditch and swallows die on the flight to Egypt.
Triumphant, O sun, hithering from nether voyage to your
  nestlings!
Yet can you not persuade the dead beloved back;
Nor time, with its magnanimous saints, counterfeit their
  vision
So that they walk here perfect before death.
                                        But Orpheus
Grieves for her still; in the shell and web of her body,
  beauty
Dreamt the forms his love made substance of and that she
  dreams in him.

Vestiges

The room dark and tight
As the core of the shut apple,
Starlight none, high up
In the skylight, townlight
Like a tall dahlia
On which smooth eyes in love
Idled for hours long,
Like in a blurred coalpit
A pin-bright vein of quartz
High in the powdery darkness,

Mouth by soundless mouth,
Like subsoil roots
Tense through worms to water.
The unsentried senses
In fenceless pit-shadow
Softly slept on guard.
Moon would have shown the beasts,
Sun the savage men.

But the door sprang to light
And police with torches
Queried the room naked,
The ogling, bogy verdict
Of a tribal justice
Dead sin resurrected . . .
False guilt, false guilt . . .

Nor did the ear hear
The desperate, friendly bells

From the depths of the breast,
With all the world's police
Round the world's love-bed.

Lakeside

The wind brushes against my heart.
Lamplight whitens the planetrees, how
Fever is dew upon the elders' brow,
Some may stay together, others part.
Breeze blows and the branches sway
Lovers and beloved gently sleep.

The limpid yacht disdains her crumbling way.
Gods in the sky, now smithies of the Good,
Now iced in astrophysics, heed our mood.
About prophetic dustbins, children play.
Breeze blows and the branches sway
Lovers and beloved gently sleep.

Ardour gone miserly in glittering art,
O musty baron above the creeping flood.
Deer fly from the hot, encroaching wood.
The happy and the true are far apart.
Breeze blows and the branches sway
Lovers and beloved gently sleep.

Translation of Exile and Other Poems by St-John Perse

Exile

To Archibald MacLeish

I

Doors open on the sands, doors open on exile,
The keys with the lighthouse keepers, and sun beaten out on the threshold stone:
Leave me, dear host, your house of glass on the sands . . .
Summer, all gypsum, whets its lance-heads in our wounds,
I have chosen a place glaring and null as the bone-heap of the seasons,
And, on all the shores of the world, the ghost of the god in smoke abandons his bed of asbestos.
The spasms of lightning are for the delight of Princes in Taurida.

II

Dedicated to no shores, imparted to no pages, the pure beginnings of this song . . .
Others in temples seize on the painted altar horns:
My fame is on the sands! my fame is on the sands! . . .
And it is no error, O Peregrine,
To desire the barest place for assembling on the wastes of exile a great poem born of nothing, a great poem made from nothing . . .
Whistle, O slings about the world, sing, O conches on the waters!
I have built upon the abyss and the spindrift and the sand-smoke. I shall lie down in cistern and hollow vessel,
In all stale and empty places where lies the taste of greatness.

". . . There were fewer breezes to flatter the Julii; fewer alliances to assist the great priestly castes.

Where the sands go to their song, there go the Princes of exile,

Where there were high taut sails, there goes the wreck more silken than a lute-maker's dream,

Where there were great military actions, there lies whitening now the jawbone of an ass,

And the rounding sea rolls her noise of skulls on the shores,

And all things in the world to her are in vain, so we heard one night at the world's edge

From the wind's militias in the sands of exile . . ."

Wisdom in the foam, O plagues of the mind in the crepitation of salt and the milk of quicklime!

I learn a science from the soul's insurrections . . . The wind tells us its piracies, the wind tells us its errors!

Like the Rider, lariat in hand, at the gate of the desert,

I watch in this vast arena signs of good omen soaring.

And morning, for our sake, moves her prophetic finger through sacred writings.

Exile is not of yesterday! exile is not of yesterday! . . . "O vestiges, O premises,"

Says the Stranger on the sands, "the whole world is new to me . . ." And the birth of his song is no less alien to him.

III

". . . There has always been this clamour, there has always been this splendour,

And like a great feat of arms on the march across the world, like a census of peoples in exodus, like a foundation of empires in praetorian tumult, ah! like an animation of lips over the birth of great Books,

This huge muffled thing loose in the world, and suddenly growing huger like drunkenness . . .

". . . There has always been this clamour, there has always been this grandeur,

This thing wandering about the world, this high trance about the world, and on all the shores of the world, by the same breath uttered, the same wave uttering

One long phrase without pause forever unintelligible . . .

". . . There has always been this clamour, there has always been this furor,

And this tall surf at the pitch of passion, always, at the peak of desire, the same gull on the wing, the same gull under way, rallying with spread wings the stanzas of exile, and on all the shores of the world, by the same breath uttered, the same measureless lamentation

Pursuing across the sands my Numidian soul . . ."

I know you, monster-head! Once more face to face. We take up the long debate where we left off.

And you may urge your arguments like snouts low over the water: I will leave you no rest and no respite.

On too many frequented shores have my footsteps been washed away before the day, on too many deserted beds has my soul been delivered up to the cancer of silence.

What more to do you want of me, O breath of origin? And you, what more would you drag from my living lips,

O power wandering about my threshold, O Beggarwoman on our roads and on the trail of the Prodigal?

The wind tells us its age, the wind tells us its youth . . . Honour thine exile, O Prince!

And all at once all is power and presence for me, here where the theme of nothingness rises still in smoke.

". . . Higher, night by night, this silent clamour upon my sill, higher, night by night, this rising of the ages in their bristling scales,

And on all the shores of the world a fiercer iambic verse to be fed from my being! . . .

So great an altitude can never annul the sheer fall from thy sill, O Seizer of swords at dawn,

O Handler of eagles by their angles, Feeder of women shrill in their iron plumes!

All things at birth bristle to the east of the world, all flesh at birth exults in the first fires of day!

And here, a great murmur is rising around the world, like an insurrection of the soul . . .

You shall not cease, O clamour, until, upon the sands, I shall have sloughed off every human allegiance. (Who knows his birthplace still?)"

IV

Strange was the night when so many breaths were lost at the crossways of the room . . .

And who is that wandering before dawn at the ends of the earth, crying out for me? Which tall repudiated girl has gone, on whistling wings, to visit other thresholds, which girl, tall and crossed in love, has gone

At that hour when the lapsing constellations, whose language changes for the men of exile, sink into the sands in search of a place of purity?

World-wanderer was her courtesan's name among the priests, in the Sibyls' green caves, and morning knew how to erase the tracks of naked feet from our sill, among sacred writings . . .

Serving girls, you served, and in vain you held out fresh

linens to catch the chance fall of one pure word.

With the plovers' complaints departed the plaintive dawn, departed the showery hyades in search of the pure word,

And on most ancient shores my name was called . . . The ghost of the god dwelt among the smoking embers of incest.

And when this day's pale substance had dried into the sands,

Fragments of beautiful stories adrift in spirals, in the sky full of errors and erring premises, went turning around to the scholiast's delight.

And who was it there that flew away? And so who was it, that night, who, against my will, stole from my stranger's lips the practice of this song?

Turn over with your stylus, on the table of the shores, O Scribe, the wax impressed with the empty statement.

Waters of the deep, the waters of the deep on our tables will wash away the year's most beautiful numbers.

And it is the hour, O Beggarwoman, when on the shut faces of great stone mirrors exposed in the caves

The celebrant, shod in felt and gloved in raw silk, with a great sweep of his sleeve wipes away the illicit signs of night.

So goes all flesh to the hairshirt of salt, ashen fruit of our vigils, dwarf rose of your sands, and the spouse of a night shown out before the dawn . . .

Ah! all is vain in the winnowing of memory! all insane among the fifes of exile: the pure nautilus of free waters, the pure mover of our dreams,

And night's poems disowned before the dawn, the fossil wing entrapped in great amber vespers . . .

Ah! let them burn, let them burn on the sand-capes, all this refuse of feather, fingernail, dyed hair, impure linen,

And the poems born yesterday, ah! the poems born one evening in the lightning's fork, what's left of them is, like ash in women's milk, but the faintest trace . . .

And I, from all winged things for which you have no use, composing a language free of usage and pure,

Now I have once more the design for a great, delible poem

V

". . . Like him who strips at sight of the sea, like him who has risen to do honour to the first land-breeze (how is his brow magnified under the helmet),

My hands more naked than at birth, and lips more free, ear to the coral reef that sounds the lament of another age,

Behold, I am restored to my native shore . . . There is no history but the soul's, no ease but the soul's.

With the achene and the anopheles, with the culm and the sands, with the frailest things, with the idlest things, the simple thing, the simple thing of here, the simple thing of being here, as day drains away . . .

On skeletons of dwarf birds the childhood of the day departs, in the dress of the Isles, and lighter than childhood on its hollow bones of seagull, of seaswallow, the wind enchants the feminine seas dressed in their scaly dress for the Isles . . .

O sands! O rosin! crimson fate closing its wing case under a great, staring eye! and on the peaceful arena, exile and its pure keys, day traversed by a green bone like a fish of the Isles . . .

Midday sings, O sadness! . . . and the wonder is announced by this cry: O wonder! and it's not enough to laugh through the tears . . .

But what is it then, O! what is it that in everything is suddenly wanting? . . ."

I know. I have seen. No one and nothing need agree!— And now day thickens like milk.

Ennui seeks out its shadow in the kingdoms of Arsace; and wandering sadness trails its taste of spurge about the world, and space where live the birds of prey falls into strange intestacies . . .

Well may the sage spy out the birth of schisms! . . . The sky is a Sahel desert where the holy caravan goes in search of rocksalt.

Many a century veils itself before the lapses of history.

And the sun buries his beautiful sesterce coins in the sands, at the rising of shadows wherein the thunder's pronouncements ripen.

O presidios under the green water! let a lustrous grass below the sea speak to us again of exile . . . and the Poet takes umbrage

At these great limestone leaves on their shelves level with the abyss, lace on the mask of death . . .

VI

". . . He who, in the midnight hours, ranges the stone galleries assessing the title-deeds of a beautiful comet; he entangles quite other laws of migration and drifting; he who, with lead, gathers the red mud of the deep to model the mask of his dream; he who, in the seaports, offers his services to adjust the yachtsmen's compasses . . .

He who walks across the earth towards the great grasslands; who gives an opinion, on the way, about the treatment of a tree grown very old; he who climbs iron towers, when the storm is spent, to dispel the dark crepe smell from the forest brambles on fire; he who, in sterile places, watches over the fate of the major telegraph lines; who knows the lie and the landing point of the submarine sheet-cables; who nurses, in a place of boneyards and sewers below the city (and it is down to the peeled bark of the earth), the reading instruments of pure seisms . . .

He who, in time of invasion, has charge of the water-systems and goes up to inspect the great filter reservoirs weary of the nuptials of dayflies; he who saves from the rioters the great fetid hothouses of the Botanical Gardens, behind the green-gold iron gates; the great Offices of the Mint, of Longitudes and of the Tobacco Monopoly; the Department of Lighthouses strewn with fables and lanterns; he who, in time of siege, makes the round of the great halls in which panoplies of phasmas and vanessas crumble away under glass; who shines his lamp on handsome troughs of lapis lazuli in which an embalmed princess, her friable bones pinned with gold, descends the reaches of the centuries, capped in her sisal hair; he who rescues from the armies that rarest of hybrids, a Himalayan bramble-rose; he who, when the State goes bankrupt, finances the uneasy splendour of the stud-farms, the great brick stud-farms tawny under the leaves, like rose-gardens of red roses under the dove-noises of the thunder, like handsome gynaecea full of fiery princes, of darkness, of incense and of male substance . . .

He who, in time of crisis, arranges for the safeguard of the tall liners held under seal, at the loop of a river the colour of iodine and dung-water (and within the limbo of stained glass, in the great saloons sheeted in oblivion, there is an eternity of aloe-green light and forever an underseas world of vigil); he who lingers in the shipyards with people of no account and on the slips the crowds have deserted, after the launching of a great hull, three years in the building; he who has the job of consigning incoming ships; and he, too, who discovers one day the very perfume of his soul in the planking of a new sailboat; he who takes over the equinoctial watch on the ramparts of the docks, on the high, sonorous comb of great dams in the mountains and on the great ocean sluices; he who feels the whole incurable breath of this world suddenly breathed out of the stench of great silos and warehouses of colonial produce, where spice and green grain swell out beneath the wintering moons like creation on its stale bed; he who declares the closure of great congresses of orography, of climatology, and it is the time for visiting the Arboretum and the Aquarium and the prostitutes' district, the gem-cutters and the courts of the great convulsionists . . .

He who opens an account in the bank for the researches of the mind; he who enters the arena of his new creation, uplifted in his whole being and, for three days, no one may look upon his silence save his mother, no one may have access to his room save the oldest of the servants; he who leads his mount to the spring and does not himself drink; he who dreams in the saddlery of a smell more intense than the smell of wax; he who, like Baber, between two great feats of arms, puts on the poet's robe to pay homage to a beautiful terrace; he who becomes absent-minded during the consecration of a nave, and there are crockets in the spandrel, like ears, walled in for the acoustics; he whose inheritance, on land held in mortmain, is the last heronry, with fine volumes on venery and on falconry; he who deals, in the town, in such great books as almagesta, portulans and bestiaries; whose solicitude is for the accidents of phonetics, the alteration of signs and the great erosions of language; who takes part in the great debates on semantics; who is an authority on the lower mathematics and delights in the computation of dates for the calendar of movable feasts (the golden number, the Roman indiction, the epact and the great dominical letters); he who grades the hierarchies in the great rituals of the language; he who is shown, in a most high place, great stones glazed beneath the insistence of flame . . .

Those are the princes of exile; they have no need of my song."

Stranger, on all the shores of the world, without audience or witness, lift to the ear of the West a shell that has no memory:

Precarious guest on the outskirts of our cities, you shall not cross the threshold of Lloyd's where your word has no currency and your gold no standard . . .

"I shall live in my name," was your answer to the questionnaire of the port-authority. And at the moneychanger's you have nothing to show but that which is suspect,

Like those great iron coinages laid bare by lightning.

VII

". . . Syntax of lightning! O pure speech of exile! Far is that other shore where the message lights up:

Two women, their foreheads signed with ashes by the same thumb; two women, at the slatted blinds, their wings upraised on the same breath . . .

Were you asleep that night, under the great phosphorus tree, O heart of prayers about the world, O mother of the Proscript, when his likeness was stamped on the mirrors in your room?

And you more swift beneath the lightning, O you more swift to spring up in answer on the other shore of his soul, companion of his strength and weakness of his strength, you whose breathing was with his forever mingled,

Will you then sit on his deserted bed, amid the shuddering of your woman's soul?

Exile is not of yesterday! exile is not of yesterday! . . . O woman! Loathe that song a Barbary bird sings beneath your roof . . .

You shall not hear the storm far off multiplying the flight of our feet but that your woman's cry in the night assault once more in his eyrie the ambiguous eagle of happiness!"

. . . Be silent, weakness, and you, beloved fragrance in the night like the very almond of night.

Wandering all over the shores, wandering all over the seas, be silent, gentleness, and you, presence, arrayed with wings at my saddle's height.

I shall resume my Numidian flight, skirting the inalienable sea. . . . No vervain on the lips, but still on the tongue, like a salty substance, this ferment of the old world.

Nitre and natron are themes of exile. Our thoughts run to action on bony tracks. Lightning lays bare to me the bed of immense designs. In vain the storm removes the bourns of absence.

Those who went on their quest to the great Atlantic Indies, those who scent the new idea in the freshness risen from the abyss, those who blow with horns at the gates of the future

Know that on the sands of exile there hiss the high passions coiled beneath the lightning's whip . . . O Prodigal in the salt and foam of June! keep alive in our midst the occult power of your song!

Like him who says to the emissary, and this is his message: ''Veiled be the faces of our women; raised be the faces of our sons; and the order is: wash the stone of your sills . . . I shall whisper low the name of the springs in which tomorrow we shall plunge a pure wrath.''

★

And the time is come, O Poet, to declare your name, your birth and your race . . .

Long Beach Island, N. J., 1941.

Poem to a Foreign Lady

"Alien Registration Act"

I

Nor sands nor straw will charm the footsteps of the ages to come, where the street was paved for you in a stone without memory — O stone inexorable and green, more so than
the green blood of the Castiles beating in your temples, foreign Lady!

An eternity of fair weather weighs upon the closed membranes of silence, and, in the depths of the abyss, the wooden house moving on its anchors ripens its fruit of lamps at noon
for the warmer brooding of new sufferings.

But the trams worn out with use which went off one evening at the turning of the street, which went off on rails to the Atlantis countries by the causeways and the ramps
and the Observatory Circles overrun with sargasso,

through the districts of fresh waters and of Zoos haunted by circus folk, through the districts of Negroes and of Asians migrating like minnows, and by the beautiful green solstices of plazas, circular as atolls,
(where one night the Federal cavalry pitched camp, O thousand heads of sea-horses!)
singing the yesterdays, singing the otherwhere, sang evil at its birth, and, on the two notes of the Cat-bird, the wooded Summer of young Capitals infested with cicadas . . . Well, here at your door, left on account for the Foreign Lady,
these two rails, these two rails—come from where?—which have not said their last.

★

''Rue Gît-le-cœur . . . Rue Gît-le-cœur . . .'' sings softly the Alien One under her lamps, and there are there the mistakes of her Foreign Lady's tongue.

II

No, not tears—had you thought so?—but that affliction of the eyes which comes to us, in the end, from an excessive fixity of the sword-blade on all embers of this world,

(O sabre of Strogoff at the height of our eyelashes!)

perhaps also, in the flesh, the thorn of a younger bramble at the heart of the women of my race; and, I quite agree, the abuse until dawn of those long cigars of widows, among the people of my lamps,

in all this noise of great waters the night of the New World makes.

. . . You that sing—it is your song—you that sing all the banishments of the world, will you not sing me an evening song to the measure of my pain? a song of grace for my lamps,

a song of grace for the vigil and for the dawn darker at the heart of the althaeas?

Of violence on earth there is given to us in such large measure . . . O you, man of France, will you not see to it that I hear, under the human season, among the cries of the martins and all the Ursuline bells, rising through the gold chaff and the powder of your Kings

a laughter of washerwomen in the little cobbled streets?

. . . Do not say there is a bird singing and that he is on my roof, dressed in fine red like a Prince of the Church. Do not say—you have seen him—that the squirrel is on the veranda, with the paper boy, the begging Nuns and the milkman. Do not say that far in the sky

a pair of eagles, since yesterday, hold the City under the charm of their noble manners.

For is there any truth in all that, which has no history or meaning, which has no truce or measure? . . . Yes, all that which is not clear and is nothing to me, weighing less with me than in my woman's bare hands a key from Europe stained with blood . . . Ah! is there any truth in all that? . . . (and what is this again, on my sill,

that green-bronze bird of suspect air which they call a Starling?)''

★

''Rue Gît-le-cœur . . . Rue Gît-le-cœur . . .'' softly sing the bells in exile, and there are there the mistakes of their foreign tongue.

III

Gods close by, bleeding gods, faces painted and shut! Beneath the orangery of the noontide lamps the vastest abyss matures. And as the flood rises to your drawn blinds, Summer, already in decline, heaving in its anchor chains,

veers towards the great roses of the Equinox as towards the stained glass of the Apses.

And it is already the third year that the mulberry fruit on

the pavements of your street makes such beautiful stains of ripe wine, such as were seen at the heart of the althaeas, such as were seen on the breasts of the daughters of Eloa. And it is already the third year that at your shut door,

like a nest of Sibyls, the abyss gives birth to its wonders: fireflies!

In Summer green as an impasse, in Summer green with such beautiful green, what third dawn, drunk with belief, opens its locust wings? Soon the high September breezes will hold counsel at the City gates, on the savannahs of airports, and in a great advent of free waters

the City will pour again into the river its whole harvest of a Summer's dead cicadas.

. . . And always there is this great glitter of glass and all this lofty suspense. And always there is this noise of great waters. And sometimes it is Sunday and through the pipes of the rooms, rising from the Atlantidean pits, with that taste of the uncreated like a breath of the other world,

there is a smell of abyss and of nothingness amidst the earth's mustiness . . .

Poem to the Foreign Lady! Poem to the Emigrant Lady! . . . Shod in crêpe or amaranth among your tall trunks not yet unfolded! O great in heart and in the cry of your race! . . . Europe bleeds at your flanks like the Virgin of the Toril! Your gilded wooden shoes were in the window fronts of Europe,

and the seven blades of vermeil of Your Lady of Anguish.

The cavalry-horses are still in the churches of your fathers, sniffing at the bronze stars on the altar grilles. And the tall lances of Breda mount guard at the family gates. But many a well-born heart has gone over to the canaille. And there was also more to be said about that sign of happiness, on your gulfs too blue,

like the gold palm-tree inside the boxes of cigars.

Gods close by, frequent gods! what rose of iron will you forge for us tomorrow? The Mocking Bird is at our back! and it is not new, this story that the Old World spreads century after century, like red pollen . . . To the muffled drums of the noontide lamps we shall again conduct many a funeral procession, singing the yesterdays, singing the otherwhere, singing evil at its birth

and the splendour of living that, this year, goes into exile out of reach of men.

But this evening of great age and great patience, in the Summer heavy with opiates and the dimness of milt, I, most solitary man, who shall deliver in the depths of the abyss the people of your lamps, having taken my way up through this high district of Hospices for the Blind, enshrouded Reservoirs and encaged valleys for the dead, walking by railings and lawns and fine Italian gardens

whose masters fled one night, terrified by a smell of the grave,

I proceed, O memory! with my free man's stride, without horde or tribe, amidst the song of the hourglasses, and my bare forehead laureled with phosphorescent bees, at the foot of the vast sky of green steel as on the floor of a sea, whistling to my host of Sibyls, whistling to my host of incredulous ones, once more in dreams I pat with my hand, among so many invisible beings,

my hound bitch in Europe who was white and, more than I, a poet.

★

"Rue Gît-le-cœur . . . Rue Gît-le-cœur . . ." softly sings the Angel to Tobias, and there are there the mistakes of his Foreigner's tongue.

Washington, 1942.

RAINS

To Katherine and Francis Biddle

I

The banyan of the rain takes hold of the City,
A hasty polyp rises to its coral wedding in all this milk of living water,
And Idea, naked like a net-fighter, combs her girl's mane in the people's gardens.

Sing, poem, at the opening cry of the waters the imminence of the theme,
Sing, poem, at the trampling of the waters the evasion of the theme,
High license in the flanks of the prophetic Virgins,

Hatching of golden ovules in the tawny night of the slime
And my bed made, O fraud! on the edge of such a dream,
Where the poem, obscene rose, livens and grows and curls.

Terrible Lord of my laughter, behold the earth smoking with a venison taste,
Widow clay under virgin water, earth washed clean of the steps of sleepless men,
And, smelled close-to like wine, does it not truly bring on loss of memory?

Lord, terrible Lord of my laughter! behold on earth the reverse side of the dream,
Like the reply of the high dunes to the rising tiered seas, behold, behold
Earth used-up, the new hour in its swaddling clothes, and my heart host to a strange vowel.

II

Most suspect Nurses, Waiting-women with veiled elder eyes, O Rains through whom

The unusual man keeps his caste, what shall we say tonight to him that sounds the depths of our vigil?

On what new bed, from what restive head shall we ravish the valid spark?

Silent the Ande over my roof, I am loud with applause, and it is for you, O Rains!

I shall plead my cause before you: at your lance-points, my share of the world!

Foam on the lips of the poem like milk of coral rocks!

And she dancing like a snake-charmer at the entry of my phrases,

Idea, naked as a sword-blade at the faction fight,

Will teach me ceremony and measure against the poem's impatience.

Terrible Lord of my laughter, save me from the avowal, the welcome and the song.

Terrible Lord of my laughter, what offence rides on the lips of the rainstorm!

How much fraud consumed beneath our loftiest migrations!

In the clear night of noon, we proffer more than one new

Proposition on the essence of being . . . O smoke-curves there on the hearth-stone!

And the warm rain on our roofs did just as well to quench the lamps in our hands.

III

Sisters of the warriors of Assur were the tall Rains striding over the earth:

Feather-helmeted, high-girded, spurred with silver and crystal,

Like Dido treading on ivory at the gates of Carthage,

Like Cortez' wife, heady with clay and painted, among her tall apocryphal plants . . .

They revived with night-dark the blue on the butts of our weapons,

They will people April in the mirrors' depths of our rooms!

Nor would I forget their stamping on the thresholds of the chambers of ablution:

Warrior-women, O warrior-women towards us sharpened by lance and dart-point!

Dancing-women, O dancing-women on the ground multiplied by the dance and the earth's attraction!

It is weapons by armfuls, helmeted girls by cartloads, a presentation of eagles to the legions,

A rising with pikes in the slums for the youngest peoples of the earth—broken sheaves of dissolute virgins,

O great unbound sheaves! the ample and living harvest poured back into the arms of men!

. . . And the City is of glass on its ebony base, knowledge in the mouths of fountains,

And the foreigner reads the great harvest announcements on our walls,

And freshness is in our walls where the Indian girl will stay tonight with the inmate.

IV

Reports made to the Aedile; confessions made at our gates . . .
Be my death, happiness!

A new language offered from all sides! a fresh breathing about the world

Like the very breath of the spirit, like the thing itself proffered,

Flush with being, its essence; flush with the spring, its birth:

Ah! the full shower of the health-giving god on our faces, and such a breeze in flower

Skimming the blueing grass, outrunning the far, far-off moving dissidences!

. . . Most suspect Nurses, O Sowers of spores, seeds and light species,

From what heights fallen, what sacred ways do you betray to us,

Like the beautiful beings at storms' foot stoned on the cross of their wings?

What was it you haunted so far that we must dream of it always, dying of our dreaming?

And of what other state do you speak so low that we cannot remember it?

Did you abandon your beds to traffic in holy things among us, O Simoniacs?

In the fresh intercourse of the spray, there where the sky ripens its taste of arum-lily and névé,

You lived with the lust-leap lightning, and in the alburnum of great lacerated dawns,

On the pure vellum scored by a divine spark, you will tell

us, O Rains! what new language the great uncial of green fire was soliciting for you.

V

Your approach was full of majesty, we knew that, men of the cities on our thin slag heaps,

But we had dreamt of more lofty confidences at the first breath of the rainstorm,

And you give us back, O Rains! to our human urgency, with the clay taste under our masks.

In higher places shall we seek memory? . . . or must we sing oblivion to the gold bibles of the lower foliage?

Our fevers painted on the tulip-trees of dream, the film on the pool's eye and the stone rolled over the well-mouth, are not those fine themes to resume,

Like roses of old in a wounded soldier's hands? . . . The hive is still in the orchard, childhood in the old tree's forks, and the ladder forbidden to lightning's lovely widowhoods . . .

Sweetness of agave and aloe . . . Insipid season of the unerring man! It is earth tired of the mind's burns.

Green rains comb their hair before the bankers' glass windows. The faces of the maiden gods will be wiped off on the warm cloths of weeping women.

And new ideas come on account to the builders of Empires at their tables. A whole silent people rises in my phrases, in the great margins of the poem.

Raise up, raise up, at the ends of promontories, the Hapsburg catafalques, the tall pyres of the man of war, the tall apiaries of imposture.

Winnow, winnow, at the ends of promontories, the great ossuaries of the other war, the great ossuaries of the white man on which childhood was founded.

And let him be fanned on his chair, on his iron chair, the man preyed on by visions that inflame the nations.

We shall never see the end of it: trailing over the far reaches of the seas, the dark smoke of history's charred exploits,

While in the Charterhouses and Leperhouses, a perfume of termites and white raspberries makes bedridden Princes rise from their wattles:

''Once, once I had a taste for living among men, but now earth breathes out its alien soul . . .''

VI

A man stricken with such solitude, let him go and hang up in the sanctuary the mask and baton of command!

I raised sponge and gall to the wounds of an old tree laden with the chains of the earth.

''Once, once I had a taste for living far from men, but now the Rains . . .''

Visitors with no message, O faceless Mimes, what fine sowings of seed were yours at the borders!

For what fine grass fires among men do you turn aside your steps one night, for what stories unfolded

Before a fire of roses in rooms, in the rooms where lives the sombre flower of sex?

Did you covet our wives and daughters behind their grating of dreams? (The attentions older women pay to younger

In secretive depths of rooms, pure offices, such as one would dream of for the palps of insects . . .)

Would you not be better, among our sons, spying out the virile, bitter smell of their war-harness of hide? (like a people of Sphinxes, heavy with numbers and riddles, disputing about power at the gates of the elect? . . .)

O Rains through whom the wild wheat invades the City and the stone highways bristle with irascible cactuses,

Thousands of new stones by thousands of new footsteps are freshly visited . . . Behind windows fanned by invisible feathers, make up your accounts, O diamond-cutters!

And the man, hard among men, in the crowd, catches himself thinking of the lyme-grass on the sands. . . . "Once, once I had a taste for living without sweetness, but now the Rains . . ." (Life rises to the storms on the wings of refusal.)

Pass by, Half-breeds, and leave us at our look-out . . . He drinks of divinity whose mask is of clay.

Each stone washed clean of street-signs, each leaf washed clean of the signs of latria, we shall read you at last, earth cleansed of the copyists' inks . . .

Pass by, and leave us to our oldest customs. May my word again go before me! and we shall sing once more a song of men for them that pass by, a song of the open for them that watch:

VII

"Innumerable are our paths and our dwellings uncertain. He drinks of divinity whose lip is of clay. You, washers of the dead in the mother-waters of morning—and it is earth still among the thorns of war—wash too the faces of the living; wash, O Rains! the sorrowful faces of the violent, the gentle faces of the violent . . . for their paths are narrow and their dwellings uncertain.

"Wash, O Rains! a stone place for the strong. At the great tables shall they sit, beneath the eaves of their strength, those whom the wine of men has not made drunk, those whom the taste of tears and of dream has not defiled, those who care nothing for their name in the bone trumpets . . . at the great tables shall they sit, beneath the eaves of their strength, in a stone place for the strong.

"Wash doubt and prudence from the path of action, wash doubt and modesty from the field of vision. Wash, O Rains! the film from the eye of the upright man, from the eye of the right-thinking man; wash the film from the eye of the man of good taste, from the eye of the man of good form; the film from the man of merit, the film from the man of talent; wash the scales from the eye of the Great Master and of the Patron of the Arts, from the eye of the just man and of the man of standing . . . from the eye of the men well qualified by prudence and modesty.

"Wash, wash benevolence from the heart of the great Intercessors, seemliness from the forehead of the great Educators, and defilement of speech from the public lips. Wash, O Rains! the hand of the Judge and of the Provost, the hand of the midwife and of the layer-out, the hand licked by the sick and the blind, and the hand low on the foreheads of men, dreaming still of reins and whip . . . with the assent of the great Intercessors, of the great Educators.

"Wash, wash the peoples' history from the tall tables of memory: the great official annals, the great Chronicles of the Clergy, the bulletins of the Academies . . . Wash bulls and charters, and the Memorials of the Third Estate; Covenants, Pacts of Alliance and the great Acts of Federation; wash, wash, O Rains! all the vellums and parchments, coloured like the walls of asylums and Lazar-houses, coloured like fossil ivory and old mules' teeth . . . Wash, wash, O Rains! the tall tables of memory.

"O Rains! wash from the heart of man the most beautiful sayings of man: the most beautiful sentence, the most beautiful sequence; the well-turned phrase, the noble page. Wash, wash, from the hearts of men their taste for roundelays and for elegies; their taste for villanelles and rondeaux; their great felicities of expression; wash Attic salt and euphuist honey, wash, wash, the bedding of dream and the litter of knowledge: from the heart of the man who makes no refusals, from the heart of the man who has no disgusts, wash, wash, O Rains! the most beautiful gifts of man . . . from the hearts of men most gifted for the great works of reason."

VIII

". . . The banyan of the rain loses its hold on the City. Wandering thing on the winds of heaven,

And so it came to live among us! . . . And you will not deny that it's all suddenly come to nothing with us.

He who would know what becomes of the rains striding over the earth, let him come and live on my roof, among the signs and the portents.

Unkept promises! ceaseless sowings of seed! And smoke-curves there on the highway of men!

Let the lightning come, ah! it leaves us! . . . And at the City gates we shall usher out

The tall Rains striding under April, the tall Rains striding under the whip like an Order of Flagellants.

But see us now delivered more naked to this smell of mould

and benjamin where the black-virgin earth awakens.

. . . It is earth fresher in the heart of the fern-brakes, the rising of great fossils flush with dripping marls,

And in the harrowed flesh of roses after the storm, earth, earth again with the taste of woman made woman.

. . . It is the City livelier in the fires of a thousand sword-blades, the flight of hawks over the marbles, sky in the fountain basins again,

And the golden sow on its column in the deserted squares. It is splendour again on the portals of cinnabar; black beast shod with silver at the lowest gate of the garden;

It is desire again in the flanks of the young widows, young widows of warriors, like great urns resealed.

. . . It is freshness running to the summits of speech, foam again at the lips of the poem,

And man, once more beset with new ideas from all sides, who surrenders to the upheaval of the great surges of mind:

"The beautiful song, the beautiful song, there, above the vanishing waters! . . ." and my poem, O Rains! which will not be written!

IX

Night come, the gates closed, what does sky-water weigh in the lower empire of the copsewood?

At the points of the lances, my share of the world! . . . And all things equal, on the scales of the mind,

Terrible Lord of my laughter, you will expose the scandal tonight in higher places.

★

. . . For such, O Lord, are your delights, at the arid threshold of the poem, where my laughter scares the green peacocks of fame.

Savannah, 1943.

Snows

To Françoise-Renée Saint-Léger Léger

I

And then came the snows, the first snows of absence, on the great linens of dream and reality interwoven; and, all affliction lifted from men of memory, there was a freshness of linen cloths at our temples. And it was at morning, beneath the grey salt of dawn, a little before the sixth hour, as in a chance haven, a place of grace and of mercy for releasing the swarms of the great odes of silence.

And all night long, unknown to us, under this lofty feat of feathers, bearing aloft the soul's vestiges, the souls' burden, lofty pumice stone cities bored through by luminous insects had not ceased growing, transcendent, forgetful of their weight. And those alone knew something of it, whose memories are uncertain, whose stories aberrant. What part the mind played in these notable things, that we know not.

None has surprised, none has known, at the highest stone frontal, the first alighting of this silken hour, the first light touch of this thing, fragile and so trifling, like a fluttering of eyelashes. On bronze revetments and on soaring chromium steel, on heavy blocks of mute porcelain and on thick glass tiles, on rocket of black marble and on white metal spur, none has surprised, none has tarnished

that mist of breath at its birth like the first shiver of a sword bared . . . It snowed, and behold, we shall tell the wonder of it: how dawn silent in its feathers, like a great fabulous owl under the breath of the spirit, swelled out in its white dahlia body. And from all sides there came upon us marvel and festival. And let there be salutation upon the surface of the terraces, where the Architect, that summer, showed us the eggs of night-hawks!

II

I know that ships in distress in this wide, pale oyster-spat thrust their lowing of deaf beasts against the blindness of men and gods; and the whole world's wretchedness calls the pilot off the estuaries. I know of strange alliances between sky and water at the waterfalls of the great rivers: white nuptials of noctuids, white festivals of may-flies. And on the vast railway-stations smoky with dawn like palm-groves under glass, the milky night begets a mistletoe feast.

And there is also that siren from the factories, a little before the sixth hour and the day-shift, above there in the great lake country, where the shipyards lit up all night stretch a long sidereal vine across the espalier of the sky: a thousand lamps fondled by the raw-silk things of snow . . . Great pearl-fields widening, great flawless pearls, are they meditating their reply at the deepest depths of the waters? — O all things there to be reborn, O you entire reply! And the vision at last without fault or flaw! . . .

It is snowing on the cast-iron gods and on the steelworks lashed by short liturgies; on the slag and the sweepings and the embankment grasses: it is snowing on the fever and implements of men—snow finer than the coriander seed in the desert, snow fresher than the first milk of young creatures in April . . . It is snowing, out there, there, out towards the West, on the silos and the ranches and the vast, unstoried plains marched over by pylons; on the layout of unborn cities and on the dead ashes where the camps were;

on the high unbroken soil, poisoned with acids, and on the hordes of black fir-trees entangled with barbed eagles, like war trophies . . . What had you to say, trapper, and your two hands discharged? And what disquieting gentleness has laid its cheek tonight upon the pioneer's axe? . . . It is snowing outside Christendom on the youngest bramble and on the newest creature. Spouse of the world, my presence! . . . And somewhere in the world where silence illuminates a larch-tree's dream, sadness raises its servant mask.

III

It was not enough that so many seas, it was not enough that so many lands had dispersed the paths of our life. On the new shore, where we are hauling in the net of our routes, a growing burden, had there to be, also, all this plain-chant of the snows to rob us of the trace of our footsteps? . . . Over the longest roads of the wide world, are you stretching the meaning and measurement of our years, snows prodigal of absence, snows cruel to the heart of women where hope wastes away?

And She whom I think of among all the women of my race, from the depths of her old age raises to her God her face of gentleness. And it is a pure lineage that her grace keeps in me. "Let us be left, the two of us, to this speech without words which is yours to speak, O you all presence, O you all patience! And like a great *Ave* of grace on our path, there sings low the pure song of our race. And for so long a time this agony of sweetness has kept vigil in me . . .

A Lady of high lineage was your silent soul in the shadows of your Cross; but a grieving woman's flesh in her old age was your living heart of a woman agonizing in all women . . . In the heart of the beautiful captive country where we shall burn the thorn, it is indeed a great pity for the women of every age whose men's arms have failed them. And who is it will lead you, in this greater widowhood, to your Churches underground, where the lamp is frugal and the bee divine?

. . . And all this time of my silence in a far country, I have watched on the pale bramble roses your worn eyes become paler. And you alone were spared that speechlessness that is like a black stone in the heart of man . . . For our years are lands in tenure which no one holds in fief, but like a great *Ave* of grace on our path, there follows us afar the song of pure lineage; and for so long a time this agony of sweetness has kept vigil in us . . .

Did it snow, this night, on that side of the world where you join your hands? . . . Here, there is great noise of chains in the streets where men go running towards their shadow. And it was not known that there were still so many chains in the world for the equipment of wheels in flight towards the day. And there is also a great noise of spades at our doors, O vigils! The hireling negroes move upon the scurf of the earth like people of the Salt Excise. A lamp

survives the cancer of the night. And a bird of pink ash, which was a burning ember all summer, suddenly lights up the crypts of winter, like the Phasian Bird in the Books of Hours, Year One Thousand . . . Spouse of the world, my presence, spouse of the world, my vigil! May the fresh breath of falsehood ravish us once more! . . . And in men is the sadness of men, but also that strength which is nameless and, at moments, that grace at which they surely must have smiled."

IV

I, only accountant, from the height of this corner room surrounded by an Ocean of snows. — Precarious guest of the moment, man without proof or witness, shall I unmoor my low bed like a canoe from its cove? . . . Those who, each day, pitch camp farther from their birthplace, those who, each day, haul in their boat on other banks, know better, day by day, the course of illegible things; and tracing the rivers towards their source, through the green world of appearances they are caught up suddenly into that harsh glare where all language loses its power.

Thus man, half naked on the Ocean of the snows, suddenly breaking asunder the vast libration, follows a singular design in which words cease to take hold. Spouse of the world, my presence, spouse of the world, my prudence! . . . And turning with the day towards the primal waters, like the traveller, at new moon, whose direction is uncertain and whose gait is aberrant, it is my design, now, to wander among the oldest layers of speech, among the farthest phonetic strata: as far as the most far-off languages, as far as the most whole and most parsimonious languages,

like those Dravidian languages which had no distinct words for ''yesterday'' and ''tomorrow'' . . . Come and follow us, who have no words to say: ascending that pure unwritten delight where runs the ancient human phrase, we move about among clear elisions, the residues of old prefixes that have lost their initial, and, preceding the master works in linguistics, we clear our new ways to those unheard-of locutions where the aspiration withdraws behind its vowels and the modulation of the breath spreads out, under the sway of certain half-voiced labials, in search of pure vocalic finals.

And it was at morning, beneath the purest of word-forms, a beautiful country without hatred or meanness, a place of grace and of mercy for the ascension of the unfailing presages of the mind; and like a great *Ave* of grace on our path, the great white rose-garden of all the snows all around . . . Freshness of umbels, of corymbs, freshness of aril under the bean, ah! so many wafers still on the lips of the wanderer! . . . What new flora, in a freer place, absolves us from the flower and from the fruit? What bone shuttle in the hands of very old women, what ivory almond in the hands of very young women

will weave us fresher linen for the burns of the living? . . . Spouse of the world, our patience, spouse of the world, our vigil! . . . Ah! all the dwarf-elder of dream against our faces! And once again, O world! may your fresh breath of falsehood ravish us! . . . There where the rivers are still fordable, there where the snows are still fordable, we shall pass on, this night, an unfordable soul . . . And beyond are the great linens of dream and all that fungible wealth in which man involves his fate . . .

★

Henceforth this page on which no more is written.

New York, 1944.

Later Poems
(1946-1959)

ST. MALO

The face of one I loved and one befriended.

Ghosts fill the dark air
Attempting to recover lost ground
Like our repentances, divine and human,
The street-lamps pad away with failing whisper.
And stars are more or less, when you look at them, like ghosts.
Pains and penalties of all men repeat,
Like the people in the Gospels
And the ghosts of the dead and the living weave through them all still.
Women vanish when their hands are tired.

In the night-bar, black and red;
And the gold on the hair of a girl entering brings back
The noon, all that placid light-veiling shadow . . .
While I weep somewhere in the distance . . .

Ah how in a blue-wind street above the sea,
Against the sun, talking and listening, she bore an idol honey-coloured, abstracted out of cell by money-yellow cell and fish-scale eyes;
All tales of childhood lead me to an idol:
Or how, the time she startled, at evening,
Out of the bloody underbrush
After the badger's death, being after being —
Being after being of light, on wings and with one sound (rising which sounded Beauty! Beauty! and falling Faith! Faith!) and out there between the sea and the sun, some love-goddess

clung like a lark to the clear air.
It was being in the making of heaven, intoned in the terrestrial
Rehearsal of the faithful, being with her,
The red-cheeked faithful, busy with hope. Yet
If in that heaven my difference should compose,
And in such temporal harmony of health and harm,
Flood of perfection flood back over me, there,
There, in that bubble I'd exaggerate
A wet miniscus of discontent,
And all my activity lie
Chaffing between diameter and arc.
Time virtual is what keeps me in Time:
Leave me in abeyance.

WELLS

Cathedral close, lawn green as a race-horse run,
Along the foot of the buttresses,
A fewscore unregulated graves.
She walked slowly, miming with her lips,
What spoke out of stone
As undeniably as a clerk walks out of a red suburban street to
his daily rubrics;
These memorials filed with the evidence
Their good deeds, their pious influence . . .
Who moves there? who does not move?
What insensate leg fails to twitch away from the mad, unphonetic works?
Catherine, it says, *Catherine*
Whom now an afflicted husband mourns.

It was before and after the needling of some old hair-splitter from
the dark.
The thing behind your elbow:

And there were two, always in soft sunlight drawn close
Together, so by the sensuality of all the particles and particulars of nature
In such an embrace of space that the thrust of sunlight in the failing wind and the lapse back of the little winds upon the sunmotes took place at the same time and the same place.

CHARTRES

The spires, firm on their monster feet rose light and thin and trembling in the tracery of bird-motion and bell-echo;
A woodshaving sailed on the calm, vernal water.
Now, fixing our secret in my eyes, that's what is there,
That's what is there, she said, all this is more
Beautiful then Chartres.
Again, again protesting
Like those who will not surrender a small liberty
Which they cannot cultivate in any case.
Rebellion is imperfection, like all matter:
Mirror with reflection, I am helpless,
As if I were watching a wooden beam pushing up through the soil
As if I were the soft-voiced people forever against the people with hard voices.

Whereas, O my term, my unavoidable turnstile
In the cathedral porch, I call you these things,
Term itself, apse itself, had you but come,
Our absolute Lord had not been me, not me or you,
But an instant preconising eternity
Borne between our open eyes,
With no perceptible bank of land between,
Nor oblique eyesight deciding other objects were there.

SCHWABING

Come back! come back! your absence loss of tears.
Come back! no cause for fear,
Youth's faithfulness with which I failed you most
Is changed now to a gentler way of seeing
So well I can be faithful to a ghost.

Mostly there's one that loves and one lets love:
But our two appetites devoured their food;
Yet join me in this company I keep:
Not life but below it or above
Where bodiless blind eyes seem to weep

Day, grey, low over the stormy wheat.
Sky parturient with rain,
And all my laughter ripped out, thrown aside,
Like the sick squads of wheat; all my gifts to her!

Rodents in the corn like the black gas in the heart of the sun.
The chase and the loving under the damp ditch;
Her blond laughter now indecent, her sexual
Ascetic face with the bones loosened.

The first rejection is the first injustice,
And inadmissable then the crisp, indifferent blow.
By turn, the flesh gone fire and the bones gone wood.
The brain stutters and stops.

I am the eldest son and my right was questioned
My patrimony drained.
I blackened with hatred,
As the trees ached intolerably through all their branches,
While the laughter was muffled

And the mud crackled round the mounting pulse.

ILE-ST-LOUIS

It goes on all night, the sorceresses whispering
Wind in the wood, and when you listen
Vanishing like a whistle downriver. Then, Oh, cling
Close to the world and her; she crowns
This moment with the diadem of her Time, and waves
The floral barge into a frame of trees;
Her eyes darken with the music,
Darkness lies against her mouth,
There is a sharp wind between laugh and cry.

Last night on the gilded Bourbon bridge
The doom of Adam brought me down to earth
While the houses with their ruined freight
Filed down the soft, erotic river.
I was not guilty, had I but known it!
For now and then the royal pall of peace
Can fall without prayer, without need,
Love's earnest gift being frivolously given;
And as the lucid, pagan music
Blows with brown leaves over the asphalt,
Guilt slips off like a wet coat in the hall.

. . . And past her ivory head
Stream the pebble notes like a run of deer;
A shy god moves across the terrace,
A being born among the flowers of her mind
Beautiful, loving and beloved.

In all these one-room flats, while the street-lamps, unseasonably

awake all night long,
Mutter their proverbs — that it's not worth it, it makes no difference —
How many white-collar clerks sit alone over a thin drink
Singing ballads out of anthologies,
Reading, in a spurt and laze, the provincial eyebrow raised,
The Essays of Sorel, the novels of Maxim Gorky! and brush their teeth,
Take two aspirins and fall between the soiled sheets,
Thinking of the good brother and sister who have stayed at home
In the country where the trucks are loading now
With greens and tuberose and cackle;
And fall asleep and resume the dream
Of the fern and roses altar in childhood,
Of the campaigns of childhood
Against the fortress of the Snow Princess.

GENEVA

My beloved is sad, my beloved lays her cheek upon her hand.
My beloved is sad, sad, my beloved is fearful for us,
"I fear for us" she says.
"Where are the masses of little liquid bells, they used to ride through the snowy curtains;
"Where are the reindeer that agitate their tresses of bells?"
And I say:
"Look out through the window again
It is the mealtime at midday
Do you see the minimum buses coming to berth at the pavements?
Do you see the experts trip gaily down the steps on helpless marionette legs across the square?
Doesn't this amuse you just as much?"

And she says:
"It does; it does; it is beyond compare; what do I care?"

The snow climbed into the white sky,
Plains of desolation above the eyes,
Each inch and acre more and more dead,
A white inexorable hound.
Lord! In the height, in the cold!
What repose to cease in the Lord
From Heaven come, what pleasure
To strip off my flesh-bound intellection
That shard which does protect, yet
Rots the heart

What head thrown back!
That I need see the equal human,
The natural surroundings of my earthly rank, breast to the sun, legs refreshed with wind
Giving in, stepping down.
But I cannot, for the heavens do not open, as far, so far as I can see.
I will kneel
My genuflection shall sign my faith like a hidalgo before his emblem,
Making her the absolute woman of a moment.

Give me your hand, let me help you over the fence.
If you touch a wire, snow will shirr up and fall round you like hundreds of eyelids closing, saying with understanding, I know, I know:
If you know, why will you try to avoid me in your flimsy heart
No more secure than net of snow?
Well you've guessed it, round tree, stone and wave . . .

That your brighteyed challenge draws me on only, your diamond moods.
Now our feet must reach the ground, our cadence into one another ineluctable,
What peaceful arms were we stilled, burning in snow!

When women leave, with the sky darkening like violets in their eyes, they step clear and look sideways, the fingers trailing over the horse's flank;
Morning calls, evening falls quiet.
Yesterday it was the flesh; fruit and flower and in the eyes concentrated all that is straight, all that dares not ignore the oblique floor of death; yesterday she being there, when it was love;
Then it was nothing more and nothing less; but now, she being gone, the more thickens and the less thins,
The more of affairs, the fattening jowl; the bow to senior and the blow to junior; the casual unwilled depths of the poem and harvest not miraculous after the sower. The father and mother, none of these
None of these: why none? And yet what's all rejection
But courage telling lies in ageing blood?

GALWAY

Nothing less it was then; and now, O warning from nowhere,
Nothing less it is now than You, there's no, no
Backing away from the invisible rider's rein;
None of these gifts or gains, or losses turned over and over
Till they shine like gains, but that divine
Dissidence in river and wheat
Wet stone, horse unharnessed
Corrupts the smile of the harvest:

And it's no use turning aside, no use
Staring through grey windows
At the bent rain
Slanting on grey seas.

As the sun stands there at one word,
And the awakened eye owns all creation:
So was she,
So was she, lord created, prisoner made,
Strong as a fortress, shining as an early fortress.

But the future like a flock of insurance clerks
Came cawing through my branches —
How long these green, ungrown and candid leaves —
How I might make my soul
In a freedom that might destroy it?
How my busy, alien eye and lip
Might graft and gratify her eye and lip
How the irritant perfect would flush out
Leaving our imperfections gape?

These questions pondering, I pulled up short
Like, against the breakwater of humanity, the shameful,
    unrealised, sad-eyed, animals
While the fiery circle cataracting outerworld
Showed in cold, peaceful stars to our little world
In its circular band of frisky, divine air
In which we build basilicas
And sicken at the sight of two-headed calves.

DUBLIN

In the memory, years interweave: they do not follow one another

Like jealous ambassadors in the Mayor's procession.
All the years flow from a hundred streets
Intemperately towards the mansion,
Last year no less than this
For her mercurial year threads through them all since;
Since her year like children:
As down an esplanade a Sunday afternoon
The two descend, assembling their anonymity
And in their mind's maze is hidden a maze with children playing
Their flat, white voices rising like kites above
Their peripatetic manoeuvers and aerial constructions
From which we are as far
As from ants in their odyssies.

But children, like the thought of flowers, come free
In the mind's upper room of luck
With furies and prophecies outside ours,
A senselessness of marionette;
But they scream, smile and flit —
Like, by a deathbed,
The multiple silence of the witness
While the testator is scoring his point over death;
Like the thought of birth and death rounding off a beautiful form;
Like heart to heart
She who was like love-children born.

The years weave through me and young men spend their time,
Evenings of unhappiness, a great weak iris . . .
Time does not stretch ahead of me
As if I might unroll my scroll on it
But it is volumed round me, thick with echoes, things
I cannot see throughout.
Such things so and so many years ago:
The already is my present unresolved.

SIRMIONE

Separate and self-absorbed, the friends grown older,
Return from the central mystery in the maze
To the primitive blaze of the virgin at the door;
And the mistresses of dead politicos, by the shining lakeside,
Fade, like the hatred in which their Chief went down;
So life both flares and fades in me without her —
Or no, not quite; when I think of a white
Dress along the battlements above the star-broken sea
Or white lips in the dark stair-well, life without her
Is reading the table of contents without the book.

This I knew,
When the children were ghosts by the lakeside,
The woman a ghost doll in the palm of my hand:
No Lady of the Sonnets, no Cathar,
No need to think of her but as separate;

No need to make of her
Any invisible, ideal vampire
Sucking my cells that water anyway.

Night is wide and without definition,
One or two recognitions, heard, spoken,
Fallen valleys of silence between,
Evening falls past the window and eyes glow.
Young men will not name the beloved object for fear of degrading
  it.
Mental prayer is the highest . . . And just at that point
Which is only, and nothing else, Yourself
Is that point, is that which I love
With no words for it.

IRVINE

Since the time in childhood
When dishes gleamed on the dresser,
And the tall, blue benignant
And black, malignant ghosts
Meant what they said,
Blue for heaven's haven,
Black for the fear of hell;

A boy on a blond crate
Outside the sunlit stables
Under sheets of silence
Spoke low to the large-eyed racehorse;
Before that Eldest Son
Had heard of the Princess,
Before the Flood
Had washed the world's kidneys,
When eyes grew brighter and brighter
And tears of generosity
Were in surprise created
Out of the musing flesh:

There spoke something else —
But the sense escaped me —
And if we were in sin,
Sad or joyful sin,
Singing or sighing
Round the corner of the eye —
Round the invisible back:
Since the time in the back field
The vast copper beech,
With the pronged sensibility
Of his thousand leaves,

Received and weaved and changed
Logical shafts of light
And modulating rain,
And through his roots, rain rising
Like a diver back;
Or from the beach at evening
The sea like a musing spider:
Both thousand leaves and sea
Sang something else,
Shone something else;

Since men can have said
On their bed of death —
"I have made women happy!"
Or, "that was in my good days,
I bred a handsome filly!"
Or, "I lowered the price of bread,
A new-elected Minister!"
Or, "with my love I loved
Those who gave their lives!"

Something there was other
Always at my elbow,
I sang, hunted and hated one;
He sings and hunts and hates me;
Say heaven or hell,
Say well or ill,
I cannot make it different,
Anything, or even other.

O day of labour!
O day of labour and of spit in which I was cast down and raised up!
When the foreign power intervened and made all the difference
Between the bog and the road,

Making the present, making life
Where the bull is silent in his shadow
And the farmhouse in its handmaid ring of trees;

There is the light small in the dark;
There is the heart filled with oil which will burn,
Which will be quenched.

The world glows with mortal divinity;
The red turns grey,
The ash creeps up on the flame
O Heavenly Foreigner! Your price is high.

NOTRE DAME DE PARIS

There is nothing now that will buy Him off;
The singers of life who are the memory of life
Are silenced by the scream of plant, tree, sea;
The beautiful severed head floats downriver;
The land recedes
With all its needy industry of wheat and vine;
With her weaving spells out of the spell of her speech,
Weaving charm out of the charm of her body;
The day recedes with all my adorations.

How she stood, hypothetical-eyed and metaphor-breasted,
Weaving my vision out my sight,
Out of my sight, out of my very sight,
Out of her sight,
Till the sight I see with is blind with light
Other than hers, other than mine;
Till it unravels
And there's only a light smoke in my hands.

And this is where, O bed of beds!
Tiger, rough of skin and smooth of eye!
She is my loss and my lost one
And I will possess and dare, cannot possess
This other one, this similar, this One.

Like all rivers with their diverse chimes hurrying towards the sea,
So all my be and are towards You.
There is none but You I think of.
I know there is one thing, which is You, it is the unique
Which also in part is she,
You, not seen by her,
You, not to be reduced by my eyes' famine of her.
She and I the Rest I absorbed in You.
And well You know it; a night like this tramps off, its footsteps small on the vast talking page it rolls its black, schoolman ruler over, five-thousand year China and then Russia and then Central European time, round and round and the world accompanied by the lights we make and the dreams closed in our humble sleep.
Well You know it, the end I mean,
It is that by which You know the anguished communication between us.
Being of my being, say of my say!
We are pulled up short by death,
Our hands make the final signal on the same high-voltage wire;
Like the mob which stampedes across a racecourse and is pulled up at the palisade, its members turning, regarding each other, surprised into violent introduction;
And know themselves — with eye and skull, with skeleton.
As I know You, there, behind my back. As I know as far as I can think and have thought You.

There is none so much as You, none You, I think of.

The Colours of Love

To my wife Caren

Women that are loved are more than loveable
    Their beauty absolute blows:
But little, like the urgent, carnal soul,
    More than its leaves so mortal in the rose.

O rose! O more than red mortality!
    What can my love have said
That made me her imagine more than be?
    Her mind more than mind, blood more than red?

As the noise of cars and chariots fades,
    And the empire of the stars
Reconquers with its bright and dusty blades
    My room, and heals my scars,

I raise my arms to that mistress planet,
    Venus, whose hunting priests explain
My heart and the rush of legend on it,
    Making me man again!

Those beautiful women shone against the dark
With flowers upon the breast, and birds
Disturbed by foreknowledge, sang some notes.
There were unshed tears, reproach and fret;
I wondered if their women's time was yet.

And the flowers like milk in a dark pantry at night
Offered themselves to the groping hand;
The cliffs fell faster than tears

Reaching that pain where feeling does not matter;
Nor through the house the ghosts' averse patter,

Repeating their old theme of the unknown
Birds or women never did translate:
It was as if eternity were breathing
Through the small breathing of the flowers
Shining upon its breast with speechless light.

Remember! do you think I could forget?
The pigeons growl like dogs in sleep remote.
Yet now if you should ask, I could not yet
Forswear that fascination, break that note

Which death in his lush garden exercised,
The habit of repentance feeds the sin,
I know that sloth the solitaries disguised,
I know the door the sweet fogs entered in.

As memory more fitful daylight makes,
Death can increase his holdings in my sleep:
While benched and cheery drunks pull up their stakes
For one more day in search of food and keep.

Abundant stone figures sun themselves
In the precarious granary of the light,
Husbanded by our father, our farmer, selves
Against subversive, supernatural blight.

Voices from the shrubbery nearby:
''Smile with your eyes,'' one says, ''what sweet invention!''
What did that Mediterranean nymph reply?
''Smile with your fables and their sweet intention.''

Listen in the gold confusion of the wheat,
Inside mortality, to what can move you:
The protests, the protection, the defeat —
''When I am gone'' the voice asks, ''who will love you?''

The crackling lightwaves overhead
Minimise our human year.
O blond haunches! O white bed!
O harmless, ultramundane fear!

Refuge of sinners! Night by night!
Bury your head beneath the sheet:
Still the unworldly angels fight
And casually tear their meat.

It cannot well be said of love and death
That love is better and that death is worse,
Unless we buy death off with loving breath
So he may rent his beauty with our purse.

But is that beauty, is that beauty death?
No, it's the mask by which we're drawn to him,
It is with our consent death finds his breath;
Love is death's beauty and annexes him.

While pestilence feathered down, the hero wasted
Nor would he ''cry aloud'' or ''breathe a prayer''
It being essential to the gall he tasted
That bitterness only bitterness can share.

How could he climb the glen through ruined farms

Nor hear his dead fathers take up arms?
He is a hero, and must make his peace
With all that's left — a few unfrocked police!

I think of seal-barking seas in the West,
It's all between a cry and a caress,
Where the windy islands yield no yeast
And men bake their own bread of bitterness;

Carry the soil of salvation in their arms
Lay it on rock and put down the seed,
It's all in a bed that chills and warms
With too much brood and too little feed.

I saw him move among the iron leaves
Which were to carbonise through his love's breast.
Hers, and the graves of lechers, louts and thieves,
Would sag and musty change be all their rest.

When leaves have fallen and there's nothing left
But plainsong from ascetic bony birds,
I say a prayer for all who are bereft
Of love, of leafy summer, of loving words.

I met a kinsman in the market-place,
Singing, and as he sang my courage grew,
It was about betrayal and disgrace,
He said "Love fails but love of love stays true."

Singing in vain and formal in the shade
The noble poverty those houses made.

Divinities of my youth,

Expound to me my truth;

Whether from Judah or Rome
Or my nearer Gaeldom.

The driven horse formalises
His speed for prestige and for prizes,

The girl swinging on the swing
Of the convent, makes me sing

And apples drop like centuries from
The tree of life, so long in bloom;

But, divinities of my youth,
You can no longer tell the truth,

It is too much a struggle to
Keep quality confined to you.

When Spring with her lambs and sea-cries rises,
Her fluent fantasy makes a mock of me;
I throw off my absolutist devices
And dissemble in the loose, resplendent sea;

Yet think on how San Juan, bitter and bare
Wrapt in his drama, sent his cry above
And though, through layer on suffocating layer
Nothing came back, he loved; and so I love.

At the Bar du Départ drink farewell
And say no word you'll be remembered by;

Nor Prince nor President can ever tell
Where love ends or when it does or why.

Down the boulevard the lights come forth
Like my rainflowers trembling all through Spring,
Blue and yellow in the Celtic North . . .
The stone's ripple weakens, ring by ring.

Better no love than love, which, through loving
Leads to no love. The ripples come to rest . . .
Ah me! how all that young year I was moving
To take her dissolution to my breast!

MR. ALLEN

From Dreghorn to the Royal and Antient Borough
Of Irvine, Mr. Allen walked my road,
I waited for him while the amber bees
Danced in the window up and down the sunlight,
Old friezecoat teacher with his violin
Under his arm, which in his mind he played;

His red Scots Guard's moustaches turning white,
He played back all his life those seven miles:
His ear was antiquarian, yet he heard
All the fledgelings fumbling in the hedgerows
Whose song I knew; and all ephemeras too.

Mr. Allen stamped into the schoolroom
From Tierra del Fuego, worlds away;
In vain seals barked in his unpublished concert —
It was before those mimes, the Elder Persons
Took on their tragic, minatory role . . .

II

Sad! to his numbered years the avid summer
Firing the hedgerows, sounded Omen! Omen!
But cool and sweet I had the room arranged:
Dark red chrysanthemums, the dead, the dead,
Like the flare above the steelworks in Kilwinning,
Like the ashes in the pipe which he put down,

He put the bow down too: I thought: "Mr. Allen, Mr. Allen,
If it's true we'll never play again together:

It's true your only heaven is in my mind!—
Even your cousin ghosts by now have left you . . .
What pain, what pride, what persiflage your life!
Teaching Glasgow brats, and then for years
With bronze translated Spaniards in the pampas,
On horseback with your pipe and violin."

THE TOMB OF MICHAEL COLLINS

To Ignazio Silone

Much I remember of the death of men,
But his I most remember, most of all,
More than the familiar and forgetful
Ghosts who leave our memory too soon —
Oh, what voracious fathers bore him down!

It was all sky and heather, wet and rock,
No one was there but larks and stiff-legged hares
And flowers bloodstained. Then, Oh, our shame so massive
Only a God embraced it and the angel
Whose hurt and misty rifle shot him down.

One by one the enemy dies off;
As the sun grows old, the dead increase,
We love the more the further from we're born!
The bullet found him where the bullet ceased,
And Gael and Gall went inconspicuous down.

II

There are the Four Green Fields we loved in boyhood,
There are some reasons it's no loss to die for:
Even it's no loss to die for having lived;
It is inside our life the angel happens
Life, the gift that God accepts or not,

Which Michael took with hand, with harsh, grey eyes,
He was loved by women and by men,
He fought a week of Sundays and by night
He asked what happened and he knew what was —
O Lord! how right that them you love die young!

He's what I was when by the chiming river
Two loyal children long ago embraced —
But what I was is one thing, what remember
Another thing, how memory becomes knowledge —
Most I remember him, how man is courage.

And sad, Oh sad, that glen with one thin stream
He met his death in; and a farmer told me
There was but one small bird to shoot: it sang
"Better Beast and know your end, and die
Than Man with murderous angels in his head."

III

I tell these tales — I was twelve years old that time.
Those of the past were heroes in my mind:
Edward the Bruce whose brother Robert made him
Of Ireland, King; Wolfe Tone and Silken Thomas
And Prince Red Hugh O'Donnell most of all.

The newsboys knew and the apple and orange women
Where was his shifty lodging Tuesday night;
No one betrayed him to the foreigner,
No Protestant or Catholic broke and ran
But murmured in their heart: here was a man!

Then came that mortal day he lost and laughed at,
He knew it as he left the armoured car;
The sky held in its rain and kept its breath;
Over the Liffey and the Lee, the gulls,
They told his fortune which he knew, his death.

Walking to Vespers in my Jesuit school,
The sky was come and gone; "O Captain, my Captain!"

Walt Whitman was the lesson that afternoon —
How sometimes death magnifies him who dies,
And some, though mortal, have achieved their race.

The Passion Of Christ

To Allen Tate

THE FALL

From what did man fall?
From the Archangel Michael's irritated wing?
Man is so small,
Without him first the universe did sing,
So fortunate since the Christ eluded his caul:
Let us take on the whole
Story in its negligence and passion —
Archangel, we your images that fall,
Dissolve and reassemble, session by session.
You rise and rise, God's wasp, and sting!
We fall and rise, God'd instrument, and sing!

THE GARDEN OF EDEN

Leaving the Graden, our first father stayed
Behind, and wept, and death is still delayed.

THE MAN OF SORROWS

He sought our sorrow out and bought it back
From merchants in the back streets of the heart:
But we, suspend between love and lack,
  Will neither sign off nor take part.

THE ANNUNCIATION

What we have best imagined is the Mother
Who, with the absolute, say Light, brought forth
Self, without intervention of the Other,
    The pure, the Virgin birth.

Gabriel, death-borne on shaking, human knees,
Humorously settles down,
Deriding with his infinite, mad eyes
    Our market risk, our saints' unknown.

THE NATIVITY

We are told how the Son of Man was born,
    Known to His Father, Who never
Recognises birth or death; and how the worn
    World's to be His breath forever.

CHRIST TAKES LEAVE OF HIS MOTHER

He, Who was born of Her that knew not Nature,
Yet with shut fists weeps like Nature's creature;
The black skies resent their shuddering wings,
And what was heavenly weeps, what natural sings.

CHRIST'S ENTRY INTO JERUSALEM

Open the gates and welcome in the Lord!
His sweet brow and invisible sword.

Now the palms wither, and the arch
Befriends no more the trulls' and porters' march.

Caesar takes the show seriously —
But Christ is serious with a world to free.

CHRIST EXPELS THE MERCHANTS FROM THE TEMPLE

The salesmen of ideas fake their list,
Worse than the trulls and their traffickers!
Again and again He strikes them off the list —
Again and again they claim the place as theirs.

WASHING OF THE FEET

With false and annual humility,
Contracting singular love into its type,
The Pharisees extend their feet, which He
In saintly rage will wash, and even wipe!

THE LAST SUPPER

None of us can remember without tears
Nor asking with what faculty we failed:
Was it the purse, or Peter's doubting ears?
    Or the rash brethren jailed?

And when Judas wiped his mouth with bread:
What horror was it raised our loyal arm?
The small room was filled with all the dead;
And Christ broke bread and broke the mortal charm.

Outside the window, the world was still,
Absence of principalities and powers:
    The world His will,
He broke bread and said He would be ours.

THE AGONY IN THE GARDEN

Peter and James and John.
Though the fox find shelter and the swollen, famished dog
And in His dispensation sleep the innocent log,
Yet the Lord finds no breast to lean upon.

Peter and James and John.
Olive branches mime against the moonlight
All natural agitation from sound to sight:
Yet there is not pain enough in Nature for Him to reason on.

Peter and James and John.
It is not angels He wants, nor fallen angels even, but men
To wear down, if only in Time, that unnatural pain;
Not active Peter, nor neutral James, nor passive John.

CHRIST BEFORE THE MAGISTRATES

By now the Church and State have had their fling,
The generous flesh is pared to the bone:
Christ and Caesar come to the same thing,
    The scorned and scornful soul, their own.

There will be something more when this is over,
The Lion and the Lamb adopt His voice,
    Beloved submit to lover,

Kneel down, and then stand up and rejoice!

VERONICA'S VEIL

They tend His fierce divinity, shy saviours,
From the calvaries of the dispossessed,
Ragged mothers who give milk to their neighbours
While the husband fails, and the child undressed

Scarbbles at the empty plate, some holy women
Will take their last white linen from the drawer
And saying: "God is ours as He is human,"
Wipe the blood from the unbearable scar.

BEFORE PILATE

To flagellate, to crown with thorns, to make
A show of man who would Man create —
Nothing much when Justice is at stake —
The conflict of laws idly becomes Fate.

The scene's complete! the filthy, wine-lit bands
Forgive Barabbas who shed blood,
Pilate, the surgeon, cleans his distant hands,
In sage disgust, praises the Good.

WAY OF THE CROSS

At every stage along that station,
Averted eyes, reluctant heart!
Mob hatred, Pharisees' elation —

His knees watery from the start,

One, Simon, in excess of passion,
Trusted his unreflecting hands;
What is this genius of compassion
That comprehends, nor understands!

AT CALVARY

Axes shone in the sunlight
Where sound and sight from one source came;
Christ was striking at the roots
Whence grew our birthright and its name,

The reason that was perfect gave
The round, simple, pagan sun:
What was humanity to save
The tears of Christ in the machine?

LIFTED ON THE CROSS

There's little certain — but no doubt
Eternity in Time's put out!

There may be lights over the plain,
That's where some acolytes, mad and sane,

Mad for life and sane for death:
Centurion! crown these ribs of wrath!

THE CROSS

Two thieves — why two? to make three criminals?
How dare the centre judge the left and right
Judging: "You shall be with Me in Paradise"
Judging: "You shall be in Hell for life"

If I were one of those two casual thieves
And spied on our degraded bloody Lord:
How coud I know how to pronounce the Word,
The Word that doubts, the Word that believes?

THE GOOD THIEF

It is not right for me to talk to You,
To wait on You with ministerial bow,
To pray, or if I lived in higher merit
To love even, or to adore, or care.
Why? the reasons? there are many of them;
    That You are there and are not there.

The huge and foreign universes round me,
The small dishonours in me coat my heart:
Whether the whim of the ignoble beast
Or the Gothic nobility of the choir,
It makes no difference, both high and low,
    Are burned to nothing in Your fire.

My will You will for a fire towards You
Dies without my kindling, or is quenched
In unguided storms from Your high quarters;
My memory in lethargy turns sour
All whence, my understanding, less imperious

Day by day and hour by hour,

Loses whole continents where in my childhood
I was Your Viceroy, and approved the Just
And condemned my natural evil thoughts —
Now, what has changed me? It is the years
You made and gave me, Lord? or am I prone to the evil
The msaters dinned into my ears?

Praise the recrimination sit well on us
Whose quality's defined by life and death;
But nothing, neither life or death adorns us
Like adoration of our Lord, the Christ,
No buildings, no culture of roses, no bridges
Like the majesty of Christ.

THE BAD THIEF

Lord, we You've made it in our power
To destroy the World You saved us in
And not only our bodies with Your souls,
Your soul created for Your praise forever
But all that has been made against Your image
Passes, both now and never,

Beasts that eat their young in innocence,
Men that torture knowing what they do —
Innocent things and conscientious things —
We who destroy the flower and the grass,
The trush whose song's as powerful as the sea
All this and more has come to pass.

ASCENSION

It happens through the blond window, the trees
With diverse leaves divide the light, light birds;
Aengus, the God of Love, my shoulders brushed
With birds, you could say lark or trush or thieves

And not be right yet — or ever right —
For it was God's Son foreign to our moor:
When I looked out the window, all was white,
And what's beloved in the heart was sure,

With such a certainty ascended He,
The Son of Man who deigned Himself to be:
Then when we lifted out of sleep, there was
Life with its dark, and love above the laws.

TRANSFIGURATION

All is as if that Face transpired with Light
As if dark were light
As if wrong were right
The torsion and the tension of that Night!

The world opens like a door: Come in!
Body is in the way,
Soul is waste and play,
Oh, come, Unworldly, from the World within!

Memoirs of a Turcoman Diplomat

OTELI ASIA PALAS, INC.

Evenings ever more willing lapse into my world's evening,
Birds, like Imperial emblems, in their thin, abstract singing,
Announce some lofty Majesty whose embassies are not understood,
Thrushes' and finches' chords, like the yellow and blue skies changing place.
I hold my stick, old-world, the waiters know me,
And sip at my European drink, while sunlight falls,
Like thick Italian silks over the square houses into the Bosporus.
Ladies, I call you women now, from out my emptied tenderness,
All dead in the wars, before and after war,
I toast you my adventures with your beauty!
Where the domes of Sinan shiver like ductile violets in the rain of light.

To the Franks, I suppose it's ugly, this brick and oblong,
When a rare sunlight, rare birdsong,
Compose the absolute kingdom far in the sky
The Franks must ask how it was known, how reached, how governed, how let die?

This woman who passes by, sideways, by your side:
There was one you loved for years and years;
Suddenly the jaw is ugly, the shoulders fall,
Provoking but resentment, hardly tears.

We all have a magic kingdom, some have two,
And cry: "O my city on the Golden Horn, and O my you!"
Discover, in the bee flaunting his black and gold among the foliage in the frieze,
You are not what you thought, you are someone like all these,
The most ardent young man turn, at the drop of a black hat,
Into some rabbity sort of clerk, some heart-affairs diplomat,
A John of the Cross into a Curia priest.

It was years ago. It is not now like when the century began —
Though apple and peach lie brilliant on the dark,
And mineral worlds on the dark sky shine,
And the red mouth breathes in: thine is mine,
And the careless Atlantic inhales the Thames, the Tagus and the Seine,
Murmuring back and murmuring forward beasts and sonata scores and Ophelian rags —
Where a girl in her balldress was a light on the wave,
Where a dying flare was like a firefly on the wave,
Where all the waves shivered with phosphorous under the moon's glacial withdrawal —
"Me voici ignorant": so a poet my father read.
The Empire born again, old pedants will rake up the dead.

My father thought my feeling could take fire by the vibrant Seine
And a tough intellect be constructed in Göttingen,
He thought, the citadels of Anatolia I could justify
Making what's hungry full, what's ragged spry.

Opalescent on the unbloodied green, the Sultan's battle
horse,
The hungry cavalry, rearing and screaming in the mist:
We put them down, these Franks, in their sweaty leather
and blasphemous curse,
Our salaried Levantine admirals sank their trading ships.
It happened: the Prophet conquered with murder in his
hand and honour in his crescent lips.

Put it down to a thick heart and a thick pate,
Such puritanic temperament's outgrown:
Now some international Secretary-General throws a lump of
bait
And laughs and says my country's not my own.

There was a professor who said: "The horse must go!"
And certain poets praised him to their shame,
Except in County Cork and Mexico
And where the quick darlings to us from the Cossacks
came.

In the Foreign Office, they humorously ask my advice,
My father had money, I was posted from place to place:
What can I tell them? even if I got it right?
There would be protocol about the right time and the right
place,
And even not too sentimental about the corps of horse
Dancing between the up-country captains' harsh knees
They could assert that horses than humanity were worse—

And that our Westernising dictator, though free was no
longer free
When at Smyrna he tumbled the chatterbox Greeks into the
sea,

Turk lieutenants, waxed moustaches and all, and spiritless mugs of tea.

WARS OF RELIGION

All is when I remember and forget
The Prophet drops the sword and shuts the Book
Down the green wind the Lord came, I met
The Lord, but did not feel or hear or look,

Interrupted by the Exarch shouting, we robbed Greece—
It's true — those comedians with their epics,
Their Aphrodite, their Achilles, their Golden Fleece,
Shouting the Prophet down, with their rational sceptics,

Even their best, their Hector, did not know,
Or mother Venus with her bog and milk,
Gesso Olympians dancing heel and toe—
Why should a Turk care about that ilk?

FOUR TURKISH WOMEN

The true, the loyal moon, not like her mother,
She was the plasma we assembled to:
All sky flows, water and blood and spittle,
Mother degraded in her human brew.

Moon! rest our emblem . . . not like Europeans
Whose stupid sun discovers all their dirt.
O Crescent, sweet and careless above the water—
Yet infidel fingers hurt

A woman, my Frankish Friend's one wife,
In a far Latin villa held his hand;
It was night all at once, and kind of grief
And kind of laughter, and kind with hand in hand.

ANATOLIA

In the high country, there is no food for ghosts,
The dead stay underground, which is their place
We had enough to do to keep the Arabs and the Bulgars in
  their place
If the dead have bad dreams, they live in us, querulous and
  lost.

Must we believe that hatred or freedom, the Sultan Ahmet
  risen on his medieval horse, turns to love?
Fail to regret the Empire, the Franks and the Hohenstaufen?
Europe and the Turk Bull?
The President of the Republic bends this way and that,
A bubble on the corner of his lips,
The Franks have their shopkeeper saints, Saint Thomas
  Aquinas,
(And Saint Thomas putting his hand in the Wound)
How can you think it's sure if you're a coward?

RISTORANT PIK NIK

The trams go tired home in the Istliqal Caddesi,
Rue du Pera, we said — The Frankish end.
The waiter flicks off a crumb. It was lamb and rice;
Would you raise your knife to stick an indifferent friend?

THE TURKISH FOR GREEK IS ROMAN

Why we call the Greeks Romans I know not
Nor without grammar do I care not:
Both were here before we were, but hear not
Nor grudge, nor love nor hate, they're lost and know not.

THE WHITE CITY

The Sava and the Danube like two horses folded, mane on
mane,
And there were dogs which lapped the water up:
Pale sunlight and pale water, as if some great poet
Said there was peace, like Goethe, and there was peace.

The sunlight pressing on the eyelids, on the waters;
Only ten years ago the invaders came,
The pretty guide talked on and showed our party—
In which were former Nazis, former Fascists—
Photo-posters of men hanging like blotting paper,
Dirty blood on dirty children, dirty mothers
The willowy waters of the Sava bathed;
Only three hundred years ago
Suleiman the Magnificent
Sick and sad outside Belgrade.

Who knows his expectations, free or slave?
Join me, Johannes, down this pretty brace:
One said, or could have sung, Come out with me,
The other, A truce to talk of genocide, and nation and race!

Tuck in your trews, Johannes, my boy, be led by me,
These girls are kind. And we're all the rage now, whiskey-

flushed men of our age,
The callow and the shallow and the fallow wiped off the page!

UNCOLLECTED LATER POEMS AND TRANSLATIONS

PALM, FROM VALÉRY

In the shadow of the blaze
Of his grace informed with dread,
An angel on my table lays
A bowl of milk, a loaf of bread;
And in his eyes reveals to me
The signal of a sacred plea
That speaks to my inner sight!
—Calm, calm, O stay calm!
Think on how the heavy palm
Carries all her breadth and height!

In such measure as she may yield
To world's abundant benefits,
Her bodily form becomes fulfilled,
Her fruitfulness her bondage is.
Oh, admirable! that vibrant head!
How she, like slow fibre-thread
Partitioning its time of growth,
Divides without let or halt
The burden of the starry vault,
The fascination of the earth!

Beautiful, moving arbiter
Between the shadow and the sun,
She simulates the sybil, her
Sleep and sagacity in one.
The same place all surrounding,
The full-blown palm accepts the abounding
Salutations and farewells . . .
What noble, what tender states!
With what good warrant she awaits

None but the god's sap in her cells!

The slight gold that is her murmur
Rings to the finger of the air,
And with plates of silken armour
Dresses the desert's soul for fair.
And the voice, time out of mind,
She gives back to the sandy wind
That sprinkles her with all its grain,
Becomes its own self's oracle,
And boasts about the miracle
Chanted by self-consuming pain.

Thus, innocent, as she reclines
Between the sky and desert floor,
Every further day that shines
Accumulates her honey store.
Her sweetness is the piecemeal ration
Of all that divine duration
Which keeps no day-book of the days,
But dissembles them instead
In a juice that brings to a head
All love's aroma, all love's ways.

If that discipline, your cult,
From time to time, thawed in despair,
In spite of all your tears default
—Save in boredom's darkened air
Yet no miser is that wise
Tree that makes and multiplies
Such gold profusion with such sway:
Through the ceremonial sap
To its fulfillment rises up
Hope that is of eternity!

These days that seem vain, all vain,
For all the universe, all lost,
Have roots that with their might and main
Labour through the sandy waste.
Substance, tough like hair created,
By dark chaos designated,
Never can its course prevent
To earth's very entrails, but
Those deep waters searches out
Which the lofty summits want.

Patience, patience be
In the blue vaults of the sky!
In each mote of silence see
The chance of its own ripeness lie!
Expect the fortunate surprise:
A dove, a light wind to rise,
The slightest variance from ease,
A woman leaning, the least strain,
Will release that blessed rain
In which we fall upon our knees!

Though a nation now collapse,
O Palm! . . . nor hope to rise again!
But down into the dust lapse
Among the shorn empyrean!
You have not lost this day and hour,
If you survive in buoyant flower
The negligence to which you bowed;
Like the man of thought whose soul
Consumes itself in growing whole
From gifts with which it is endowed!

PARSIFAL, FROM VERLAINE

Parsifal has overcome the Lemans,
Their pretty babbling and amusing lusts,
And his own virginal boyhood's fleshly leanings
Teased by their pretty babbling and light breasts;

Overcome the Woman, beautiful, subtle-hearted,
Spreading her breast and fresh arms,
Overcome Hell; he strides into the tent
A heavy trophy on his boyish arm;

The lance that pierced the side of the Most High;
He cured the king and now is king himself,
Priest of the Essence, that Most Holy Treasure;

In gold robe, he adores the glory, the sign,
The chalice in which glows the Real Blood,
—Oh, all that children's singing from the Minster!

Nineteen Poems by Char, with Jackson Matthews

WIND AWAY

Camped on the hillsides near the village are fields of mimosa. During the gathering season, it may happen that, some distance away, you meet an extremely sweet smelling girl whose arms have been busy during the day among the fragile branches. Like a lamp with a bright nimbus of perfume, she goes her way, her back to the setting sun.

To speak to her would be sacrilege.

The grass crushed beneath her slippers. Give her right of way. You may be lucky enough to make out on her lips the chimera of the damp of Night.

THE BASKET-WEAVER'S LOVE

I loved you, I loved your face, like a well-spring ravined by storms, and the secret of your domain enclosing my caress. Some rely on a round imagination, like the earth. For me going is enough. I brought back from despair a basket so small, my love, it could be woven of willow.

YOUTH

Far from the ambush of roofs and the alms of country shrines you take your birth, hostages of the birds, O fountains. Man's decline in the nausea of his ashes, man's struggle with his vindictive providence, not even these can disillusion you.

Praise, praise, we have come to terms with ourselves.

"If I had been mute as the trusty stone step beneath the sun heedless of its wound sewn with ivy," she said, "if I had been childlike as the white tree receiving the fright of bees, if the hills had lived on into summer, if the lightning had opened its gates to me, if your night had forgiven me . . ."

Eyes, the orchard of stars, the gorse, the solitude are not part of you. A song finishes exile. The lamb-wind brings back new life.

LIVING

Pass.
The sidereal spade, in other times,
Plunged and was swallowed up here.
To-night a whole village of birds
Passes over, exulting.

Hear, in the stony head
Of presences gone,
The word that will make your sleep
Warm like a September tree.

See, they tremble, the intertwining
Certitudes that have come
Among us to their quintessence,
O my Crossroads, my anxious Thirst!

The bitterness of living prowls
Ceaselessly lusting after exile.
Under a thin almond rain,
Gentle and in liberty,
Alchemy your nurse was born,
O my Love!

POSTSCRIPT

Stand you away from me who wait nor speak;
I was born at your feet but you have lost me;
Too well my flames have marked their kingdom out;
My treasure sank that struck your chopping-block.

The desert where the one firebrand took refuge
Has never called me out, nor given me up.

Stand you away from me who wait nor speak:
The clover of passion is iron in my hand.

In the dazed air through which I go my ways,
Time will clean up my face, little by little,
Like a horse aimless at his bitter ploughing.

HYMN IN A LOW VOICE

Hellas! broad shore of a sea of genius from which the breath of knowledge and the magnetism of intelligence arose at dawn, swelling with equal fertility forces that seemed endless, you are, further back, an atlas of strange mountains: a volcano chain that smiles at the magic of heroes, at the serpentine loves of goddesses, and guides the nuptial flight of man, free at last to know himself a bird and die a bird; you are the answer to everything, even to the usury of birth, even to the ways of the labyrinth. But you, mass of earth made of the diamond of light and snow, earth incorruptible beneath the feet of a people victorious over death but mortal as proof of purity, there is a foreign belief that would chastise your perfection, thinking to stifle the murmur of your wheat.

O Greece! mirror and body three times martyred, to imagine is to restore you. Your healers are in your people and your health is in your right. Your blood incalculable, I call upon it, the only living thing for which liberty has ceased to be sickly; it breaks open my mouth, the blood with silence, I with a shout.

LILY OF THE VALLEY

I stood guard over their fate, that couple. I stood by them in their dark fidelity. The aged mountain stream had read me its page of thanksgiving. A new storm was coming. The light of the earth brushed against me. And while on the window-pane the childhood of the justicer was being written (clemency being dead), my patience exhausted, I broke down in sobs.

MARTHA

Martha whom these old walls cannot take over, fountain reflecting my lonely monarchy, how could I forget you since I do not have to remember you: you are the present, accumulating. We shall come together without having to approach or prepare for each other, as two poppies in love make a giant anemone.

I will not enter your heart to shorten its memory. I will not engage your mouth so that it cannot open to the blue air and thirst for departure. I want to be freedom for you, and the wind of life crossing the threshold of always before night becomes undiscoverable.

TO THE HEALTH OF THE SERPENT

I

I sing the heat that is like a new-born babe, desperate heat.

II

It is bread's turn to break man, to be the beauty of daybreak.

III

He who believes in the sunflower will not meditate in the house. All thoughts of love will become his thoughts.

IV

Within the swallow's loop, a storm searches, a garden grows.

V

There will always be a drop of water to outlast the sun, without shaking the sun's ascendancy.

VI

Bring forth that which knowledge would keep secret, knowledge with its hundred corridors.

VII

That which comes into the world to cause no trouble

deserves neither respect nor patience.

VIII

How long will man's failure last, this dying at the centre of creation because creation has dismissed him.

IX

Each house was a season. The town in this way repeated itself. Together the inhabitants knew only winter, in spite of their heated bodies, in spite of the day that would not go.

X

You are in essence always a poet, always at the height of your love, always hungry for truth and justice. It is doubtless a necessary evil that you cannot be so, assiduously, in your conscience.

XI

You shall make of the non-existent soul a man better than her.

XII

Look how your country glows in the light of daring; this pleasure for a long time has not been yours.

XIII

Many there are who wait till the reefs lift them over

and the goal passes them by, to clarify themselves.

XIV

Be thankful to him who cares nothing for your remorse. You are his equal.

XV

Tears despise their sympathizer.

XVI

The depth remains measurable where the sands subdue destiny.

XVII

My love, it matters little that I was born; you come into sight where I disappear.

XVIII

Would I could walk, without deceiving the bird, from the heart of the tree to the ecstasy of the fruit.

XIX

That which calls to you through pleasure is nothing but the mercenary gratitude of memory. The presence you have chosen bids no farewells.

XX

Stoop only to love. If you die, you still love.

XXI

The glooms in which you steep yourself are still subject to your lusty, solar sovereignty.

XXII

Have nothing to do with those in whose eyes man is only a passing shade of the colour lying on earth's tormented back. Let them reel off their long protestation. The red of the poker and the glow of the cloud are one.

XXIII

It is unworthy of the poet to puzzle the lamb, to invest himself with its fleece.

XXIV

If we live in a lightning flash, it is the heart of eternity.

XXV

Eyes that thought to create the day, but woke the wind, what can I do for you, I am oblivion.

XXVI

Poetry is of all clear streams the one that lingers least about her reflected bridges.
Poetry, life's future held in man requalified.

XXVII

A rose that it may rain. At the end of innumerable years, that is your wish.

THE METEOR OF THE 13th OF AUGUST

Black will be that night when, in the absence of truth, man will suppress the superstition of truth.

The three phases of the meteor correspond to the three fates or, if you prefer, to the three *crossed* ways along which our life springs forward, pauses, and burns out, life almost completely deprived of free will. These describe three sovereign states, but it is impossible to say which has especial precedence, as each gives the illusion of being the most deeply, the most desperately and the most joyously felt, in equal measure and *almost* at once. In the following brief paragraphs, we have attempted a domification which, unfortunately, can only be approximate.

(THE METEOR OF THE 13th OF AUGUST)

The very moment you appeared to me, my heart had the whole sky to light its way. It was mid-day in my poem. I knew anguish was asleep . . .

(NOVAE)

The first ray, trembling between a curse under torture and magnificent love.

The optimism of philosophy is no longer adequate.

The light on the rock shelters a major tree. We are advancing to where it is visible.

Ever wider the marriage of eyes. The tragedy that is unfolding will rejoice even at our limits.

Danger wiped out our melancholy. We spoke without looking at each other. Time held us together. Death avoided us.

Larks of the night, stars, circling about the springs of surrender, be progress to these sleeping heads.

I jumped out of my bed bordered with hawthorn. Barefooted, I talk to the children.

(THE MOON CHANGES GARDENS)

Where am I to rid me of this legacy of excrement that escorts me like a lamp?

Tentative hymns! hymns denied!

Woman, mad and to the night obedient — star.

Storm liberty in the swaddling-clothes of thunder, over the supremacy of the void, in the small hands of man.

Don't daze yourself with tomorrows. What you are looking at is winter striding over wounds, gnawing at the windows; and on the porch of death, the inscrutable torture.

Those that sleep in wool, those that run in the cold, those that offer mediation, those that are not ravishers for want of something to do, are in accord with the meteor, the cock's enemy.

I have the illusion of being at the same time in my soul and outside it, far beyond the window pane and yet against it, a burst saxifrage. My desire is infinite. Nothing obsesses me but life.

Nomad spark dying in its conflagration.

Give yourself to love, O dweller by the riverside. Spend your truth. The grass that hides the gold of your love will never know the frost.

On this earth with its dangers, I marvel at the idolatry of life.

May my presence, that stirs in you a secret malaise, an unremitting hatred, be a meteor in your soul.

A birdsong surprises the branches of morning.

TO AN IMAGE OF WARRIOR ARDOUR

Our-Lady-of-Lights alone on your rock, at odds with your church, friendly to her rebels, we owe you nothing but a little charity.

I have sometimes detested you. You were never naked. Your mouth was unclean. But I know now that I was wrong, for those that kissed you had fouled their table.

Transients that we are, we have never insisted on sleep until we were tired out. Protectress of endeavour, you bear no mark, save that of those who showed you little love.

You are the moment of a revealed lie, the bludgeon befouled, the guilty torch. I have the strength of heart, fool that you are, to strike you or take your hand . . . It is for you to defend yourself.

Too many clever fools are watching you, waiting for you to take fright. You have no choice but complicity. The awful disgust, having to obey their orders, and in return serve as their ally.

I have broken silence because they have all gone and left you nothing but your clump of pines. Ah! run down to the road, make friends for yourself, be woman, but yielding woman . . .

The world has been through so much since your coming that it is nothing but a pot of bones, a will to cruelty. O faded Lady, bold shameless country girl, the lights are cold where men are born.

FLUSHED WITH JOY, THOSE THAT RISE IN THE MORNING . . .

Evidence and its near-hits are collective. Truth is personal.

Take care: all men are not trustworthy.

A welcome for him who comes to me in labour and sweat, saying: "I have come to deceive you."

O, great black helm, on your way to death, why should it always be your task to point out the lightning?

I

The state of mind of the rising sun is gladness in spite of the cruel day and the memory of night. The hue of dried blood becomes the redness of dawn.

II

Those whose mission is to arouse, begin by taking a morning wash in the river. The first enchantment and the first shock are for one's self.

III

Force your luck, clasp your happiness, and go to meet your risk. Seeing you, they will get used to your doing so.

IV

At the height of the storm, there is always a bird to comfort us. The unknown bird. It sings, and flies away.

V

The wise thing is not to collect in the mass but, in common nature and creation to seek out your number, your reciprocity, your differences, your passage, your truth, and the small bit of despair that is its goad and moving fog.

VI

Go straight to the essential: don't you need young trees to rebuild your forest?

VII

Intensity is silent. Its image is not. (I like the man who dazzles me and then accentuates my inner darkness.)

VIII

How this world suffers in becoming the world of man, shaped between the four walls of a book! That it should then be given over to speculators and fools who urge it on faster than it can go, — how are we not to see in this more than bad luck? To fight at all cost against that inevitable end with the help of our own magic, to make endless forays along the route, or what we use for the route, that is the task of the Morning people. Death is but a sleep complete and pure, with the plus sign for pilot to help it cleave the wave of becoming. Why take fright at your alluvial condition? Quit taking the branch for the trunk and the root for the void. That is at least a beginning.

IX

You must breathe on sparks to make a good light. Beautiful burnt-out eyes will complete the offering.

X

Woman, fear-inspiring, with madness in her bite and a mortal cold in her body: that knowledge which, born of a noble ambition, in the end finds its measure in our tears and our subjugation. Make no mistake, O best of men whose strong arm she covets and whose weakness she lies in wait for.

XI

When we feel the pressure to break with our luck and our courage, and to accept the various simplifications, something that owes nothing to man, but wishes us well, exhorts us: ''Rebels, rebels, rebels . . .''

XII

The personal adventure, the abundant adventure: community of our mornings.

XIII

Conquest and the unlimited preservation of the conquest *that lies ahead of us* murmuring of our shipwreck, deflecting our disillusion.

XIV

We have the peculiarity sometimes of swaying when we walk. Time is light, the ground agreeable, our foot turns where it knows.

XV

When we say: *the heart* (and say it regretfully), what we mean is the smouldering heart, clothed in our common, miraculous flesh, which can at any moment stop beating and giving.

XVI

Between *your* greatest good and *their* least bad, poetry flares.

XVII

The swarm, the lightning, and anathema: three slopes of the same mountain.

XVIII

To stand firmly on the ground and give your arm to a love unacceptable to those who sustain you, to build what you think is your house without that first stone, which will always inconceivably be missing, that is *the curse.*

XIX

Do not complain because you live nearer death than mortals do.

XX

We seem to be born always half-way between the beginning and the end of the world. We grow up in open rebellion, almost as furiously against what draws us on, as against what holds us back.

XXI

Imitate men as little as possible in their enigmatic passion for tying knots.

XXII

Death is not detestable except in the way it attacks each of our five senses one by one, then all of them together. If need be, hearing could ignore her.

XXIII

We can build *multiformly* only on error. This is what allows us to think, at each renewal, that we are happy.

XXIV

When the ship sinks, her sails find harbour inside us. Her masts rise out of our blood. Her fresh impatience gathers strength for further obstinate voyages. Is it not so, you, who are blind upon the sea? Staggering through all that blue, O sadness rising on the farthest waves?

XXV

We are passers-by *schooled* to pass by, and therefore to sow disturbance, to impose our heat, to speak our exuberance. That is why we interrupt! That is why we are untimely and unusual! The plume we flaunt means nothing. Our usefulness is directed against the employer.

XXVI

I can despair of myself and keep my hope in You. I have fallen from my brightness, and you do not notice death, in plain view, bracken in the wall, woman walking by my side.

XXVII

Finally if you will destroy, let it be with nuptial implements.

DIVERGENCE

The horse with the narrow head
Has beaten down his enemy,
The poet with the lazy heels
Knows winds more masterful
Than those that breathe in his voice.
The devastated earth recovers
Though wounded by an endless sword.

Go back in patience to your farms;
Over the almond-trees in Spring
Youth and age pour in streams.
Death smiles at the edge of Time
Giving it some nobility.

It is upon the heights of summer
That the poet's revolt begins,
And it is from the harvest's fire
He draws his madness and his torch.

THE ADVICE OF THE LOOK-OUT

Fruit springing beneath the knife
Beauty whose echo is a taste,
Dawn with your pincer jaws,
Lovers the world would pull apart,
Woman in your apron,
Nail scratching on the wall,
Desert! Desert!

PYRENEES

Mountains of the great and wronged,
On your feverish tower-tops
The last light fades.

Naught but the void, the avalanche,
Grief and regret!

Those troubadours, crossed in love,
Watched their kingdom bitter-sweet
Turn white in one summer.

Ah! inexorable the snow
Would have them at its feet in pain,
Would have them die in ice
Who have lived among the sands.

ON LEAVE

The ogre that is everywhere:
On her face you're waiting for
And in your longing for that face,
In the migration of the birds,
Beneath their feigned tranquillity:
The ogre that serves us all
And is never thanked,
In the house you built yourself
Despite the migraine of the wind;
The ogre, hooded a chimera;
Ah! if he were free to tell us
That he is the serving man of Death,

Our anguish would become resigned
But what a desert were the mind.

NIGHTS OF FULFILLMENT

With a stronger wind,
A lamp less dim,
We should reach the wayside halt
At which night will say ''Pass on'';
And we shall know it's true
When the glass goes black.

O earth all tenderness!
O branch my joy grows on!
The maw of heaven is white.
What's shimmering there is you,
My fall, my love, my prey.

FULLY

When our bones had touched land,
And through our faces crumbling come,
My love, nothing ended there.
Love came freshly in a cry
Reviving and restoring us.
Though our heat was silenced,
Something there kept on
(Different from dying life)
Unfolding to infinity.
That which we had seen afloat
Edge to edge with grief
Was there, as in a nest,

Its two eyes bringing us
Together in new-born consent.
Despite the wool of swaddling-clothes
Death had not grown up,
And happiness not yet begun
Was listening for us;
The grass was bare and trampled on.

WHEREFORE YIELD?

Oh! Woman discovered, our wings go side by side
And high heaven is their faithful air.
But what is that still shining above us?

It is the dying reflection of our daring.
When we have made our way through it,
We shall distress the earth no more:
We shall see each other.

ABEL

Who was it loved me in the Bible times?
It was my brother, best of Father's brood.
He led me through the hot, inhuman wood
And told me tales of our far Father's crimes,

I in the rear, the elder in the van:
Until he found out murder for the better;
I learnt the law, the spirit and the letter,
The handcuffs and the flail, the fall of man:

Until the bright seed burst! And world was waste;
My Father, wretched, blamed my brother Cain
Who cried: "The world is waste, the world is vain,
Bloodshed and seed, how bitter to the taste!"

Notes to the Poems

NOTES

The following notes are largely textual in character. A good part of what they record will be of use only to a reader with access to library facilities; indeed many details can only be followed up in Dublin, at the National Library. They are nonetheless offered in the belief that they indicate the most profitable route to a better understanding of Devlin's poems.

A complete register of the different drafts and stages of revision of each poem is not appropriate. I have instead recorded details which bear on the version printed as the text. Manuscripts and typescripts are located in the Devlin Collection of the National Library unless otherwise indicated. The National Library material was received in two instalments during 1988. It has still to be checked and properly catalogued, and meanwhile readers should beware that several drafts are contained in the wrong bundles.

The blue notebook, which Brian Coffey refers to in his article, "Of Denis Devlin" (9, 12), is not (yet) in the National Library, and the beginnings of poems cannot be accurately dated until it comes to hand. The typescript versions of poems are often accompanied by carbons, which I have not recorded unless they contain emendations. Nor have I recorded the typescripts made for Brian Coffey's posthumous collection. I have only recorded printings in Devlin's lifetime - viz. not in the posthumous *Selected Poems* and *Collected Poems,* in issues of periodicals like *The Lace Curtain* and in several anthologies. These later printings are part of the story of DD's reputation, and are not relevant here.

Spelling has been regularized to conform to the English norms used by Devlin, and minor printing errors silently corrected. Punctuation, on the other hand, derives from the editions and texts cited.

ABBREVIATIONS USED IN THE NOTES

"About the Poetry"	Brian Coffey "About the Poetry of Denis Devlin" *Poetry Ireland* (N.S. Dublin) No. 2 (Spring 1963) 76-86
BC	Brian Coffey
Cont	André Breton "Four Poems" translated by Denis Devlin *Contemporary Poetry and Prose* (London) Nos. 4-5 (August-September 1936) 82-5
CP	Denis Devlin *Collected Poems* ed Brian Coffey (Dublin: The Dolmen Press, 1964)

DD	Denis Devlin
Int	Denis Devlin *Intercessions* (London: Europa Press, 1937)
LD	Denis Devlin *Lough Derg and Other Poems* (New York: Reynal and Hitchcock, 1946)
MS (or MSS)	Holograph manuscript (or manuscripts)
NLI	National Library of Ireland, Dublin. Denis Devlin Papers
"Of Denis Devlin"	Brian Coffey "Of Denis Devlin: Vestiges, Sentences, Presages" *University Review* (Dublin) II: 11 (1963) 3-18
PI	Special Denis Devlin Issue of *Poetry Ireland* (Cork) No. 10 (July 1950), reprinting versions of twelve poems from *LD* and also of *The Heavenly Foreigner*
Poems	Brian Coffey and Denis Devlin *Poems* (Dublin: Printed for the Authors by Alex Thom & Co., September 1930)
SP	Denis Devlin *Selected Poems* ed Allen Tate and Robert Penn Warren (New York: Holt, Rinehart and Winston, 1963)
Thorns	Paul Eluard *Thorns of Thunder. Selected Poems* ed George Reavey (London: Europa Press & Stanley Nott, (1936))
TS (or TSS)	Typescript (or typescripts)
UCD	University College Dublin

INTERCESSIONS

On the background to the printing of *Int*, and for a suggestion that DD might have subsidized its printing, see Thomas Dillon Redshaw "George Reavey's Europa Press 1935-1939" *Linen Hall Review* (Belfast) V:1 (Spring 1988) 8-14. Texts are taken from *Int*, though I have corrected misprints with reference to other versions.

The volume was reviewed by Thomas McGreevy "New Dublin Poetry" *Ireland Today* (Dublin) II:10 (October 1937) 81-2; Anon *The Times Literary Supplement* 23 October 1937 p. 786; George Every *The Criterion* (London) XVII (1938) 338. Also, besides Beckett's *transition* essay cited in the Introduction footnote 18, see A. Rivoallan *Littérature irlandaise contemporaine* (Paris: Hachette, 1939) 125-6.

MS beginnings headed *Presentiment* assume a poem in four parts: I Dejection, II Surprise, III Hope, IV Dejection. An early MS, in which the first paragraph reaches almost its present form, and revised early TSS, are headed *Secret*. The NLI papers also include a French translation.

Death and Her Beasts, Ignoble Beasts (no.2).. 49

The earliest MS is untitled; the subsequent MS and TS are headed *Temptation*. The first published version of the poem in *Ireland Today* (Dublin) II:5 (May 1937) 34 differs from the present version in one line and is more lightly punctuated.

Victory of Samothrace (no. 3).. 51

The original holograph is dedicated to Anne Adams, and dated Munich, May 1931; another TS fragment is dated Paris, April 1933. The NLI contains other drafts and revised TSS, and the poem was first published in *The Dublin Magazine* IX: 4 (October-November 1934) 5-6. The periodical version is not divided into paragraphs, and the line-divisions are varied almost adventitiously, as if to adjust to the page-width. Reprinted in *LD* (no. 70 below).

The Statue and the Perturbed Burghers (no. 4)...................................... 54

A first, heavily corrected and added-to TS, is headed *Adventure*; a second TS is headed *Romance Sentimentale*; a third TS has the present title. (*Adventure* is the generic title of a number of MS poems dating from the early thirties, which DD never published as a group or sequence. For other poems which developed from this group, see nos. 59, 62, 64 and 68 below). Reprinted unchanged in *Maryland Quarterly* No. 2 (1944) 34 and, with different punctuation, in *LD* (no. 40 below).

Windtacker Windjamming (no. 5).. 55

An early MS and two different TSS are headed *Tacking*; a carbon of the second TS is signed and dated Paris 1933; and the title of another is changed to *Windtacker Windjamming*. Three further TSS bear the present title. Compare on no. 69 below.

Liffey Bridge (no. 6).. 57

The beginnings of the poem might be preserved in the MS drafts, fair copies and revised TSS of *Chanson de France*, dated Paris 1933, containing *The Unready, Liffey Bank* and *Intercession in Behalf of Good Men*. There is also a corrected TS of the present poem, with the present title added, and three later, heavily revised TSS of the same.

Gradual (no. 7)... 60

Two early MS drafts and four TSS all bear the present title.

Daphne Stillorgan (no. 8)... 61

The first two MS drafts are headed *Summer Morning,* the third *Country Station,* the fourth is untitled. A subsequent TS with the present title is signed and dated Paris 1933; and further TSS contain corrections. Reprinted in *LD* (no. 66 below).

In the Last Resort (no. 9).. 63

The earliest MS drafts are headed *The Abandoned Scaffolding,* and the NLI also has a series of drafts of a related, longer poem headed *Street-Organ* (once *Beggar's Suite),* a fair copy of which is signed and dated Paris 1933. Two early TSS are headed *In any Case,* and signed and dated Dublin 1934. Subsequent TSS and carbons, some revised and added to, bear the present title.

Bacchanal (no. 10).. 64

The first notes and drafts and revised fair copy, dating from 1933, are headed *News of Revolution*: this early version was published by Brian Coffey in *Advent. Denis Devlin Special Issue* (Southampton) No. 6 (1976) 22-4. The early TSS and carbons of *Bacchanal* are heavily revised. Reprinted in *LD* (no. 58 below).

Communication from the Eiffel Tower (no. 11)...................................... 69

The first holograph draft and corrected carbon are headed *Presentiment 1932*. The first of a series of three revised TSS, which also date from Paris 1932, is headed *Presentiment of 1940,* and the third bears the present title. Two further corrected TSS are extant.

BC relates the poem to DD's interest in dreams and in surrealism, and says the poem ''draws everything from one dream'' (''About the Poetry'' 81-2). The French ethnologist, Count Gobineau, mutates into German Gobethau in the same way that his *Essai sur l'ineqalité des races humaines* (1853-55) was distorted by Nazi programmes for the purity of the Aryan race. F. -N. Babeuf (1760-97), radical democrat in Revolutionary France whose particular interest in land distribution earned him the nickname Gracchus, was frequently appealed to by later left-wing activists. The final line ("IN SOME 8 YEARS.' ") is illuminated by the earlier titles.

Entry of Multitudes into an Eternal Mansion (no. 12)............................ 80

Five different TSS, some of them with carbons and several annotated, all bear the present title.

Est Prodest (no. 13)... 82

The materials which embody the first stages of the poem are in private hands. These materials comprise a series of early MSS, TSS and revised TSS in which the poem developed and enlarged through four distinct stages. Some MS beginnings, along with TSS and carbons (one corrected, lightly), are also held in the NLI. The difference between the final revised TS and the version published in *Int* are very slight. Further revisions were made in *LD* (no. 47 below), which again occupies a crucial position in the collection as a whole.

Argument with Justice (no. 14).. 88

Two pages of prose notes and a MS first-draft precede eight different TS versions, several with multiple carbons, the two earliest of which are corrected. Reprinted in *LD* (no. 55 below).

The Lancet (no. 15)... 90

There are five TS versions, one corrected, all with the present title. Reprinted in *LD* (no. 71 below).

UNCOLLECTED EARLY POEMS AND TRANSLATIONS

Prayer to Our Lady, from Le Cardonnel (no. 16)................................ 94

Published in *Missionary Record of the Oblates of Mary Immaculate* (Dublin) XXVII: 1 (January 1929) 4, signed Denis Devlin, where no more particular ascription than "(*Translation*)" follows the title. MS drafts are headed *Laus, Daily Bread* and *Prayer to our Lady,* and a MS fair-copy identifies the author of the original. The NLI also has a TS.

Compare *Prière du soir d'été* in Louis Le Cardonnel (1862-1936) *Poèmes* (first published in 1904) (Paris: Mercure de France, 1925) 174-5.

O Paltry Melancholy (no. 17).. 96

Published in *Poems* 6. There are two revised holographs, the second dated 15 July 1930, and two later TSS.

BC describes the background to *Poems* in ''Of Denis Devlin'' 4; though his suggestion that DD had ''completed'' only four poems needs to be interpreted in a particular sense.

Before Lepanto: The Turkish Admiral Speaks to his Fleet (no. 18)............... 98

Published in *Poems* 9-10. There are two early holographs, the first (untitled) dated 26 July 1930, and two later TSS.

Adam's House (no. 19).. 100

Published in *Poems* 14-6. Following a collection of notes and phrases, there are two early holographs, the first signed and dated September 1930 and the second an unsigned, undated fair-copy; also two later TSS.

Now (no. 20).. 103

Published in *Poems* 18-20 (I have corrected two misprints). Stanza 1 appears on the verso of a MS poem entitled *To a Pure Maid,* which was written in November 1929. A holograph of the complete poem, under the title (*Contrapuntal* del.) *Decay | By Thogorma,* is written on UCD Dramatic Society paper; and there are two later TSS.

The poem was first published in *The National Student* (Dublin) N.S. I:2 (January 1930) 121, under the title *Decay,* where it provoked an unsympathetic response in the next number by S. Ó Cionnaith (I:3 - December 1930 - 142-4).

Passerelle, trans. Bonheur (no.21).. 106

Published in *14, rue du Dragon* (Paris) No. 3 (mai 1933) 12, ''par Denis Devlin *Traduction de Gaston Bonheur''*. I did not find DD's original English version among the NLI material, but I could have missed it. The French version (tr *Gangway)* shares themes and images with *West Pier, Est Prodest* and *Ballad of Mistress Death* (nos. 46, 13/47 and 49). French versions of other poems are recorded in the notes to no. 1 above and no. 77 below.

Bonheur (b. 1913) went on to a distinguished career in publishing, as well as becoming the author of novels, biography, plays, song-lyrics and verse. See BC on DD and Bonheur, in ''Of Denis Devlin'' 6.

The Investiture of D'Artagnan (no. 22).. 107

Published in *The Dublin Magazine* N.S. XI:3 (July-September 1936) 4. A signed holograph fair-copy is dated 1935, though BC remembers the poem from *circa* 1930 (''About the Poetry'' 80). There are also three TSS, each differently revised. An earlier version of no. 74 below also uses the persona of D'Artagnan.

D'Artagnan is the young Gascon who comes to Paris and is admitted to the *Corps des Mousquetaires* at the court of Louis XIII, in Alexandre Dumas' famous novel.

She of Always, All of Her, from Éluard (no. 23)................................ 109

Published in *Thorns* 5. The NLI has a corrected TS. Compare *Celle de toujours, toute* in Paul Éluard *Oeuvres complètes* (Paris: NRF/Gallimard, 1968) I 196-7.

Thorns was published in June 1936, when the International Surrealist Exhibition opened in London, and other translators included Samuel Beckett and David Gascoyne. BC comments on DD's critical interest in surrealism in ''About the Poetry'' 81-4 and ''Of Denis Devlin'' 12. DD's translations are from two of Éluard's collections, *Capitale de la douleur* (1926) and *La Vie immédiate* (1932). The NLI has MS translations of six further Éluard poems from *La Vie immédiate,* in various stages of completion, besides the poems included here (nos. 23-7 below).

Nakedness of Truth, from Éluard (no. 24).. 110

Published in *Thorns* 6. The NLI has a holograph MS. Compare *Nudité de la vérité* in Éluard 149.

Girls in Love, from Éluard (no. 25).. 111

Published in *Thorns* 39. The NLI has a holograph MS. Compare *Amoureuses* in Éluard 303.

One for All, from Éluard (no. 26).. 112

Published in *Thorns* 44-5. Compare *Une pour toutes* in Éluard 397-8.

They are Alike, from Éluard (no. 27).. 114

Published in *Thorns* 47-8. Compare *Les Semblables* in Éluard 381-2.

The Vertebrate Sphinx, from Breton (no. 28).................................... 116

Published in *Cont* 82-3. The NLI has a corrected TS. Compare *Le Sphinx vertébral* in André Breton *Poèmes* (Paris: NRF/Gallimard, 1948) 88-9.

The Plume, from Breton (no. 29)... 118

Published in *Cont* 83. The NLI has a corrected TS. Compare *L'Aigrette* in Breton 41-2.

Allotropy, from Breton (no. 30).. 119

Published in *Cont* 84. The original poem appears not to have been collected by Breton.

Rather Life, from Breton (no. 31) 121

Published in *Cont* 84-5. The NLI has a corrected TS. Compare *Plutot la vie* in Breton 37-8.

Na Leannáin, from Nerval (no. 32).. 123

Published in *Ireland Today* (Dublin) II:3 (March 1937) 44, along with no. 33 below. The holograph MS is in the NLI. Compare *Les Cydalises* in Gérard de Nerval *Oeuvres complètes* (Paris: NRF/Gallimard, 1960-84) I 26-7.

Besides the five poems which were published in *Ireland Today* (Nos. 32-6), the NLI has MSS and TSS of up to fifty further translations of poems by modern French poets into Irish, in various stages of completion. A preliminary list in DD's hand divides the project between himself and Niall Montgomery, but the evidence of the MSS suggests that the project turned out differently - DD making the translations, Montgomery revising them -, unless DD's holographs derive from earlier drafts or dictation by Montgomery. *CP* xvii-viii summarizes the project and quotes Montgomery's later comment.

Tórramh, from Rimbaud (no. 33)... 124

Published on the same page as no. 32 above. Compare *Veillées* in Arthur Rimbaud *Oeuvres complètes* (Paris: NRF/Gallimard, 1972) 138-9. Lacking MS or TS evidence, it is impossible to tell whether DD meant not to translate the last two lines of the French or whether their omission is a printer's error.

An Áille, from Baudelaire (no. 34)... 125

Published in *Ireland Today* (Dublin) II:3 (March 1937) 52 under the French title *La Beauté,* along with no.35 below. Compare Charles Baudelaire *Les Fleurs du Mal* (Paris: NRF/Gallimard, 1972) 49.

Leoithne Gaoithe Muirí, from Mallarmé (no. 35)............................... 126

Published on the same page as no. 34 above, under the French title *Brise Marine.* The Irish title is taken from the TS version. Compare Stéphane Mallarmé *Oeuvres complètes: Poésies* (Paris: Flammarion, 1983) 176.

Amhrán an leannáin mhí-ámharaigh, from Apollinaire (no. 36)............. 127

Published in *Ireland Today* (Dublin) II:8 (August 1937) 27-8, under the French title *La Chanson du mal-aimé.* The holograph MS is in the NLI. Compare Guillaume Apollinaire *Œuvres poétiques* (Paris: NRF/Gallimard, 1965) 46-8.

LOUGH DERG AND OTHER POEMS

The volume is dedicated "TO ADRIENNE". Adrienne Koch (b. 1912) won the Woodbridge Prize in Philosophy at Columbia in 1943 with the publication of her Ph.D. thesis, *The Philosophy of Thomas Jefferson.* She went on to pursue a distinguished academic career, and published books on Jefferson, Madison, John Adams and others. Text are taken from *LD,* though I have corrected misprints with reference to other versions.

The volume was reviewed by Anon *The New Yorker* XXII:23 (20 July 1946) 75-6; Marguerite Young "New Volumes of Verse in Review" (with others) *New York Times* 21 July 1946 Section 7, p. 12; Babette Deutsch "A Learned Craftsman of Verse" *New York Herald Tribune Book Review* XXII:49 (28 July 1946) 3; Selden Rodman "Daemonic Poet" *The New Republic* (New York) CXV:4 (29 July 1946) 106-7; Richard Lattimore "Three Poets from across the Water" (with others) *Accent* (Urbana, Ill) VI:4 (Summer 1946) 268-70; Arthur Mizener "Poets" (with another) *The Nation* (New York) CLXIII:6 (10 August 1946) 160-1; Austin Clarke "Local Talent" (with others) *The Irish Times* 17 August 1946 p.4; Randall Jarrell "The Poet and his Public" (with others) *Partisan Review* (New York) XIII:4 (September-October 1946) 488-500 (492-3 especially); Valentin Iremonger "Less Than Passion" *The Bell* (Dublin) XIII:2 (November 1946) 165-7; Inez Boulton "Celtic Nova" *Poetry* (Chicago) LXIX:3 (December 1946) 169-71; Pearse Hutchinson "Denis Devlin. A Review" *Irish Bookman* (Dublin) I:6 (January 1947) 23-6; Dudley Fitts "Eleven of An Unkind" (with others) *Quarterly Review of Literature* (New Haven, Conn) IV:1 (1947) 92-8 (96-7 especially). At least two reviewers (Deutsch and Jarrell) developed or revised their comments in subsequent book-length publications.

Lough Derg (no. 37).. 132

Early jottings which contain phrases used in the poem suggest it began as a satire on urban life and creeping worldliness, not as a poem about the Irish place of pilgrimage. Later, whole stanzas are mixed up with the MSS of *Laputa City* or *Wishes for Her With and Without Her*, a poem dating from DD's first years in America, about New York City (the *Lough Derg* page has marginal notes: "For A. K.", "To A. K.", "To Adrienne"). Differently, three further pages of lines and jottings contain four stanzas which make up an ending which is more directly critical than the present one: the poet cannot pray like the humble women because his prayer would be mocked by theirs, be merely narcissistic.

There are twelve different TSS of the complete poem under its present title. The three first are heavily revised (one supplemented with a page of MS revisions), four contain lighter revisions. The poem was first published in *The Southern Review* (Baton Rouge, La) VII:4 (Spring 1942) 856-9, and details of the phrasing and punctuation of nearly every stanza were revised when it was collected.

DD visited Lough Derg in Donegal with his mother when he was fifteen or sixteen (William G. Downey "Thinking of Denis Devlin" *Éire-Ireland* - St. Paul, Minnesota — XIV:1 - Spring 1979 - 102-14 107 especially). It is a particularly severe pilgrimage, whose long and contentious history has most recently been reviewed in the introduction and bibliography to the translation by J.-M. Picard and Y. de Pontfarcy of a famous twelfth-century account, *Saint Patrick's Purgatory* (Dublin: Four Courts Press, 1985). The island and its cave, during the early middle ages, came to be associated with St Patrick's descent to Purgatory. Pilgrims flocked to the place from all over Europe, including it is said, Dante, who derived the idea of the Divine Comedy from his experience (compare stanza 10). Its only rival among places of pilgrimage in Christendom was Santiago de Compostella, and in the seventeenth century it was the subject of a play by Calderon.

Irish people have continually resisted attempts to suppress or demystify the pilgrimage by Church and State. It is celebrated in different ways by Thomas Moore ("I wish I was by that dim Lake" in *Irish Melodies*), William Carleton, and W. M. Thackeray *(Irish Sketch Book*, 1843). In the present century, it has been the occasion of poems by Patrick Kavanagh *Lough Derg* (written 1942; published 1971) and Seamus Heaney *Station Island* (1984). Robert Welch "Language as Pilgrimage: Lough Derg Poems of Patrick Kavanagh and Denis Devlin" *Irish University Review* (Dublin) XIII:1 (Spring 1983) 54-66 develops one such comparison.

Encounter (no. 38.. 136

The original untitled holograph is written on the verso of some

(American) logic exercises. The five different TSS differ hardly at all. The poem was first published in *Accent* (Urbana, Ill) IV:2 (Winter 1944) 72 (followed by nos. 44 and 60 below). Details were improved in each stanza when the poem was collected in *LD*, especially in the phrasing of stanza 3.

From Government Buildings (no. 39).. 137

The MS and the first of six different TSS (the first four corrected) do not bear a title. The poem was first published in *Briarcliff Quarterly* (Briarcliff Manor, NY) II:7 (October 1945) 65-6, and only punctuation was changed in *LD*.

The Statue and the Perturbed Burghers (no. 40)...................................... 139

See no. 4 above. Reprinted with only changes of punctuation from *Int*.

Memo from a Millionaire (no. 41).. 140

The first MS draft (on New York University writing paper) is in prose; the second is titled *God and Mammon*; and a corrected TS, with MS additions, is titled *Uncut Transcription of a Picture by Georges Braque* (a title shared with a MS *Adventure*, among DD's unpublished poems). There are three different TSS, the first called *Memo for a Millionaire* and the two later ones bearing the present title. The poem was first published in *Maryland Quarterly* No. 1 (1944) 2-3. Three changes of wording and some changes of punctuation were made when it was collected.

Royal Canal (no. 42).. 142

The four TS versions differ only slightly. The two earlier ones are given the title of another Dublin location - *Mespil Road* - and one of these is corrected. The revised title adjusts the social pretensions downwards, makes the pathos less comfortable. Reprinted without change in *PI*.

Mixed Drinks (no. 43).. 143

Two of the four TSS contain some MS revisions, but the four versions in fact differ very little.

Jansenist Journey (no. 44)... 145

The original MS is headed *Adventure*. The NLI also has an untitled TS, and three further TSS - one corrected for the *LD* volume. The poem was published in *Accent* (Urbana, Ill) IV:2 (Winter 1944) 72-3 (along with no. 38 above and no. 60 below). Phrases were changed in stanzas 6, 8 and 9 when the poem was collected, as well as punctuation, and *LD donkey's* replaces the earlier plural *donkeys'*. *PI* reproduces the *LD* text, with *it* for *his* in stanza 9, which appears to be a mistake.

Casa Buonaroti (no. 45).. 147

There are five TS, three of them corrected. The earliest TS is headed *Renaissance Maker*, the second *Casa Buonarroti, Florence.* This second, corrected TS is endorsed by DD: "Sent Dublin Magazine, March 1st 1942", but the poem was first published in *LD*. The "he" of the poem is of course Michelangelo.

West Pier (no. 46).. 148

Of the four TS versions, the first three contain extensive MS revisions and drafts. The poem was first published in *Calendar. An Anthology* (Prairie City, Illinois: The Press of James A. Decker, 1942) 9-10 (along with nos. 53, 59, 73). Stanzas 3, 4 and 6 were rewritten and expanded for the *LD* text, which was reprinted in *PI.*

The West Pier is the less salubrious of the two arms of Dun Laoghaire harbour, which of course fail to unite. Joyce's description in *Ulysses* of a pier as a failed bridge might also be recalled.

Est Prodest (no. 47).. 150

See no. 13 above. The *Int* text was revised for *LD* - with passages being rewritten, added to, removed.

Handy Andy (no. 48).. 156

The three TS versions show only slight variations of punctuation and phrasing, and none is corrected.

Ballad of Mistress Death (no. 49)... 157

The four TSS all differ slightly in punctuation and phrasing. The first has the title inserted in pencil, but none is corrected. The poem was first published in *Briarcliff Quarterly* (Briarcliff Manor, NY) III:9 (April 1946) 43; when it was collected two slight verbal changes were made (in stanzas 1 and 3), and, oddly, punctuation was omitted (for which there is support in the TSS). The *LD* text was reprinted in *Contemporary Irish Poetry* ed Robert Greacan and Valentin Iremonger (London: Faber and Faber, 1949) 37-8 (with no. 56 below); also in *PI* (which omits line 26).

Ank'hor Vat (no. 50).. 159

The two holograph drafts are untitled; the four TS versions, two of which are corrected, are very close to one another. The poem was first published in *University of Kansas City Review* X:2 (Winter 1943) 117. The *LD* version differs in running together two paragraphs as one, in the phrasing of two lines and in removing punctuation.

Angkor, now in Cambodia, was the capital of the Kmer Empire which dominated South East Asia between the ninth and twelfth centuries. It was dominated by vast architectural monuments, among which the temple complex of Angkor Wat was one of the most imposing. The city was abandoned to the jungle by the sixteenth century, but largely recovered by French archaeologists from the nineteenth century onwards.

DD's spelling of the title might suggest a French source; indeed, St-John Perse served and travelled in the region at the beginning of his diplomatic and literary career. The title in the 1943 publication was contained entirely in quotation marks. Angkor Wat might be thought to bear more than a passing resemblance to Washington DC.

On Mount Muckish (no. 51).. 161

There are seven TS versions, the early ones being considerably corrected and rewritten. The first title was *Ancestral,* changed to *Come Full Circle;* a version called *On Muckish Mountain* is marked as having been sent to *The Dublin Magazine* on 3 March 1942 (where it was not published); later versions are headed *On Mount Muckish.*

Muckish, "The Pig's Back", presides over the North Donegal landscape more noticeably than nearby Mount Errigal, which is better known from postcards. DD had family connections with the region.

Meditation at Avila (no. 52).. 162

The untitled first draft is in prose, in several sections, written in pen and pencil and evidently continued and revised at different times. A heavily corrected TS (verse) is titled *Meditation at Avila,* and has a motto from Pascal: "Console-toi! tu ne me chercherais pas si tu ne m'avais pas déjà trouvé." Three of the four TSS have corrections. The poem was first published in *The Sewanee Review* (Sewanee, Tenn) LII:4 (October 1944) 530-3. The *LD* printing incorporates a few, minor verbal revisions, adds punctuation and changes spelling.

BC records that DD visited Spain perhaps only once, for three weeks during Spring 1932, but that the country made a deep impression on him

(''Of Denis Devlin'' 5-6). A recording of DD reading the poem is extant, in which he introduces the poem as follows: ''The scene is at Avila, which of course is the native and dwelling town of St Teresa of Spain. The speaker is supposed to be standing in the city looking out of the window, over the wild Castilian plateau, and he is talking to his soul which is given a special connotation here. The conversation is supposed to build up a role for the soul which is a mixture of consciousness and persistence.'' (Reading at Young Men's Hebrew Association, New York City, 3 January 1945; recording in Library of Congress Archive of Recorded Poetry and Literature, 1966 Checklist No. 197/LWO 2529).

Old Jacobin (no. 53).. 167

The original holograph (in pencil, corrected in ink) is headed *Fugitive Statesman,* as are two subsequent corrected TSS. A third TS with two carbons, all three corrected, is headed *Robespierre at Charenton.* Two further TS versions, the second further revised, are headed *Old Jacobin.* The poem was first published under the title *Fugitive Statesman* in *Calendar. An Anthology* (Prairie City, Illinois: The Press of James A. Decker, 1942) 5-6 (along with nos. 46, 59, 73).

In the version collected in *LD,* besides the change of title, the poem is differently divided and the lines in each paragraph are considerably rewritten. With the shift from the new Irish Republic to the French, the poem becomes more dramatic even as it becomes more extreme; it becomes more exclamatory and elliptic, and the speaker is meanwhile distanced from what is spoken more vividly. Apropos of the evocations of the Shannon in the early version and the note on no. 54 below, it might be remarked that de Valera was from Limerick.

Anteroom: Geneva (no. 54).. 169

Two TSS are titled *Antecamera: Geneva 1938,* the second being corrected to *Anteroom: Geneva 1938;* a third TS is titled *Anteroom: Geneva.* The poem was first published in *New Republic* (New York) CIII:18 (28 October 1940) 596 under the first of these titles. When it was collected in *LD,* several isolated verbal improvements were made in addition in providing the final title.

For what it is worth, DD frequently accompanied Eamon de Valera to meetings of the League of Nations in Geneva at the time the poem is dated. The two developed a liking for one another which is described by Mervyn Wall *Éire Ireland. Weekly Bulletin of the Department of External Affairs* (Dublin) No. 493 (5 September 1960) 10; *Advent. Denis Devlin Special Issue* (Southampton) No. 6 (1976) 19-20. Compare on no. 53 above.

Argument with Justice (no. 55).. 170

See no. 14 above. The *Int* text was reprinted unchanged in *LD* - apart from punctuation and spelling and the plural breasts in line 7. I have emended the line 7 reading since it has no support in any of the TSS.

Pays Conquis (no. 56).. 172

The five different TSS differ only in details, and only one contains a (minor) emendation. There is also a carbon of the version first published in *New Republic* (New York) CIII:18 (28 October 1940) 596; and further carbons of the version collected in *LD*. Two lines were amended for the *LD* volume, and some slight additions and alterations of punctuation were also made. The *LD* version was reprinted in *Contemporary Irish Poetry* ed Robert Greacen and Valentin Iremonger (London: Faber and Faber, 1949) 37 (with no. 49 above); also in *PI*.

Boy Bathing (no. 57).. 173

Two early MS drafts are headed *Boy Bathing*. There is also a TS headed *Boye Bathynge*, in which the text of the poem is spelt in antique, and a TS headed *Moments*, signed Dublin 1934, in which the present poem is no. II (untitled), no. I being an unpublished poem elsewhere called *Girl Whirling*. Four TS versions of the poem with its present title differ only in small details; one is corrected. The first TS is endorsed "Published *Irish Times*", but I have not located the poem there. Reprinted in *PI*.

Bacchanal (no. 58).. 174

See no. 10 above. The *LD* text differs from *Int* in the phrasing of four lines, and has heavier punctuation.

After Five o' Clock (no. 59).. 179

There are four TS versions, the first headed *Adventure* being accompanied by two other unpublished sets of lines with the same title. See above no. 4 on DD's *Adventure* project; also nos. 62, 64 and 67 below. The poem was published under its present title in *Calendar. An Anthology* (Prairie City, Illinois: The Press of James L. Decker, 1942) 11 (along with nos. 46, 53, 73). One word was changed, and some punctuation, when the poem was collected in *LD*.

Annapolis (no. 60).. 180

There is a corrected MS, and four TS versions and carbons, with only a few minor corrections. The poem was first published in *Accent* (Urbana, Ill) IV:2 (Winter 1944) 73-4 (along with nos. 38 and 44 above). When the poem was collected in *LD,* small changes were made in each paragraph and the last paragraph was rewritten as a whole.

Some of the background of the poem is provided by William G. Downey (see note on no. 37 above) 110-1.

Tantalus (no. 61).. 182

The original MS draft is untitled; a TS is headed *You Can't Have It Both Ways;* and there is a further TS. When the poem was first published in *Ireland Today* (Dublin) I:7 (December 1936) 33 (along with no. 63 below), it was under the title, *Lord, I Can't Have It Both Ways.* When it was collected in *LD,* two phrases were changed *(loathed the yoke* for *left her folk; till* for *until),* and it was given its present title and punctuation. The *LD* text was reprinted in *PI.*

The Blind Leading the Blind (no. 62).. 183

An early corrected TS is headed *Adventure II* (there is also a corrected carbon). See no. 4 above on DD's *Adventure* project; also nos. 59, 64 and 68. These are followed by a TS to which DD added trial titles, as follows: *The Blind Leading the Blind, The Gap of Danger, On Howth Head, The Height of Caution, Gothick Fool.* Then there are two different untitled TSS, one corrected; then a corrected TS headed *The Blind Leading the Blind;* then two carbons of a further revised version, headed *The Blind Leading the Blind.*

Freedom No Object (no. 63).. 185

The original MS draft is in pencil; it is followed by three TS versions. First published in *Ireland Today* (Dublin) I:7 (December 1936) 33 (along with no. 61 above). Punctuation (only) was added when the poem was collected in *LD.*

Celibate Recusant (no. 64).. 186

The earliest TS is headed *Adventure* and signed Dublin, October 1934. (For DD's *Adventure* project, see no. 4 above; also nos. 59, 62 and 67.) A later TS and carbon, both corrected, are headed *You Don't Know a Good Thing When you See It,* and there is another TS with the same title: the title in all three cases is deleted, and *Celibate Recusant* substituted. Two different TSS are headed *Celibate Recusant.* The poem was published under the title *You Don't Know a Good Thing When You See It* in *transition* (Paris) No. 25 (Fall 1936) 9. When it was collected in *LD,* one word was changed (*Fool* for *slave),* punctuation was added, and the poem was given its present title.

Obstacle Basilisk (no. 65).. 188

There are three TS versions; the earliest is extensively revised, the second less so. Reprinted in *PI*.

Daphne Stillorgan (no. 66).. 189

See no. 8 above. The *LD* text differs from *Int* in the phrasing of three lines and in punctuation.

Welcome My World (no. 67).. 191

The earliest (corrected and signed) TS is not titled; a corrected TS is headed *Invitation;* two other TSS, with carbons, are headed *Welcome My World* and contain minor corrections. After publication in *LD,* the poem was reprinted without change in *An Anthology of Irish Verse* ed Padraig Colum (New York: Liveright, 1948) 343-4; and in *PI.*

Summer Jujube (no. 68).. 193

The earliest MS draft is headed *Extrahuman Adventures I;* the second MS and the first two corrected TSS are headed *Adventures I.* For DD's *Adventure* project, see above no. 4; also nos. 59, 62 and 64. The title of the first TS is corrected to *Summer Jujube,* which is the title of three other TS versions.

Poet and Comic Muse (no. 69).. 195

A MS and two early TS versions (one corrected) are headed *Actress Attracting;* in another TS, *Acress Attracting* continues on from *Windtacker Windjamming* (no. 5 above). Three TS versions (one corrected) are headed *Poet and Comic Muse.*

Victory of Samothrace (no. 70).. 196

See no. 3 above. The differences between the *LD* and *Int* texts are continuous with earlier revisions: that is, there are improvements of phrasing and further adjustment of line-divisions.

The Lancet (no. 71).. 199

See no. 15 above. *LD* adds punctuation to the text of *Int*, Americanizes the spelling and, in line 2, changes *Int goldfinches* to *goldfishes* (both readings are supported by several TSS).

Venus of the Salty Shell (no. 72).. 202

A pencil draft on the verso of Washington writing paper is not titled, but two TS versions (one corrected) are headed *Aisling*. Three further TS versions bear the present title.

Edinburgh Tale (no. 73).. 203

A MS version is untitled, but an early corrected TS has the pencilled-in title *Can You Meet Me To-Night?* which is carried forward to a second corrected TS. Three further TS versions, one corrected, are headed *An Edinburgh Tale*. The poem was first published under the later title in *Calendar. An Anthology* (Prairie City, Illinois: The Press of James A. Decker, 1942) 7-8 (along with nos. 46, 53 and 59 above). The title reached its present form when the poem was collected in *LD*; also, phrases were clarified throughout and more paragraph divisions were inserted.

Between the Late and Early (no. 74).. 205

A MS version is untitled; an early TS version is headed *Listen Here to Me*; three further TS versions bear the present title. The early TS is close to the version published under the title *D'Artagnan Makes a Case!* in *Ireland Today* (Dublin) II:11 (November 1937) 34. Compare no. 22 above for another poem which uses the persona of D'Artagnan. The version of the poem collected under the present title in *LD* has different punctuation (which makes a difference to the prose-sense of line 11) and a differently - phrased ending. The *LD* text was reprinted in *PI*.

Eve in My Legend (no. 75)... 206

Among the severally-filed MS beginings in NLI, the two earliest are headed *The Muse*. The earliest MS beginnings of the poem in its present form, and the two earliest TSS and a holograph fair-copy, are nevertheless untitled. Three different sets of TSS try different titles - *Second Sight* and *Evening, With Excitement* - before the present one was arrived at.

Wishes for Her (no. 76) 208

A MS draft and corrected early TS are untitled; there is also a TS bearing the present title.

Little Elegy (no. 77) 209

Two early corrected TSS are untitled; the title is written into a third TS version, and included in three further ones, two of which are corrected. The poem was first published in *Ireland Today* (Dublin) II:3 (March 1937) 33-4; then, with a few verbal improvements, in *Calendar: An Anthology of 1940 Poetry* ed Norman MacLeod (Prairie City, Illinois: The Press of James A. Decker, 1940) 14-15 (DD read the poem at the Young Men's Hebrew Association, Lexington Avenue at 92nd Street, New York, on 6 May 1940). When it was collected in *LD,* further slight improvements of phrasing were made, as well as refinements in punctuation. A French translation, *Petite Elegie,* is among the papers at the NLI.

Brian Coffey has written an answer-poem, *Syllables for Accents* (*Selected Poems* - Dublin: New Writers' Press, 1971 - 60 - 1).

Picture in a Window (no. 78) 211

The earliest draft, in pen and pencil, is untitled; but a fair copy is headed *Elegy Written in the Classical Manner*. A revised, signed holograph, dated Dublin, September 1931, is headed *For Brian* (sc. *Coffey*). *Picture in a Window; being an elegy in the classical manner.* This is followed by a heavily-revised TS bearing the title, *Elegy on a Picture in a Window*, emended to *Picture in a Window: Hylas & the Nymphs* and with the present motto for the first time. Three sets of TSS/carbons mark further stages in the development of the poem under its present title.

Farewell and Good (no. 79) 213

The reworked MS draft is untitled. Four successive TS versions follow, containing MS revisions, each headed *Farewell to Her.* Following further MS reworking, the poem went through three more revised TS versions under its present title. It was first published in *Poetry* (Chicago) LVII:5 (February 1941) 300 - 1. When it collected in *LD,* the phrasing of ten lines was further improved, and a few changes made in punctuation.

Love from Time to Time (no. 80) 215

There are several MS beginnings, in pen and ink, on different kinds of paper, all untitled. All but one of the five different TS versions, two of them corrected, bear the present title. One TS is annotated in DD's hand, "Published *Calendar*", but I have not been able to discover if the poem was published here before it was collected in *LD*. For *Calendar*, published by James A. Decker, see on nos. 46, 53, 59, 73 and 77 above.

A Dream of Orpheus (no. 81) 217

The drafts and revisions are especially plentiful. Among a clutch of notes, MSS and corrected TS drafts, one of the earliest MSS is headed by the opening lines of Rilke's first four *Duineser Elegien* (a holograph translation of the beginning of the first, into English prose, is among DD's papers). The verse lines which follow in the same MS are headed 'ΟΡΦΕΥΣ ΕΥΡΙΔΙΚΗ

The various early verse drafts are very different from the final poem; and prose notes and verse fragments suggest a range of themes which was afterwards taken up and developed fully in *The Heavenly Foreigner.* Two of the three TSS of the completed poem are extensively revised.

Vestiges (no. 82) 220

The five different TSS - the earliest not titled, another corrected - differ very little. The *LD* text was reprinted in *100 Modern Poems* ed Selden Rodman (New York: Pellegrini and Cuhady, 1949) 159-60; and in *PI.*

Lakeside (no. 83) 222

The two-page early MS is not titled. Thereafter, two TSS are headed *Song;* two subsequent TSS, *Lake Geneva;* a TS which introduces the refrain for the first time, *Dark Ages;* and only the last TS, *Lakeside.* There is a further corrected TS related to the version headed *Song,* and all TSS except the last are heavily revised.

TRANSLATION OF EXILE AND OTHER POEMS BY ST-JOHN PERSE

Exile, Poem to a Foreign Lady, Rains, Snows (nos. 84-7) 224

St-John Perse (pseud. Alexis Leger), permanent secretary at the French Foreign Office, arrived in New York in 1940, in exile from his diplomatic career. He began a series of poems which broke almost two decades of silence as a poet, in which he explored new ground. The poems were published in American and other journals, beginning with *Exil* in *Poetry* (Chicago) in March 1942.

DD's translation, *Rains,* was first published, by itself, in *The Sewanee Review* (Sewanee, Tenn) LII:4 (October 1944) 483-92. The translation, *Snows,* was first published, facing the French text, in *The Sewanee Review* LIII:2 (April 1945) 186-97. Both translations were separately reprinted in signed, limited editions, both with the French text *en face,* by *The Sewanee Review* in 1945. The translation, *Poem to a Foreign Lady,* was published following the French text in *Briarcliff Quarterly* (Briarcliff Manor, NY) II:8 (January 1946) 214-21 (217-21).

All four translations were published together - that is, including DD's *Exile* for the first time - under the title *Exile and Other Poems* (New York: Pantheon Books, Bollingen Series, 1949). This was a large-format volume which included the French texts *en face,* and also notes by Archibald MacLeish, Roger Caillois and Alain Bosquet. A second edition in smaller format, without notes, was published in 1953; and this was reprinted in 1962.

The way in which the translations were done is described by DD in the memoir referred to in the Introduction (footnote 8: the holograph MS and the TS are in the NLI collection). Some letters DD wrote to Perse are now in the Fondation Saint-John Perse at Aix-en-Provence; as well as offprints of *Rains* and *Pluies* annotated by the French poet. The annotated and revised TS of *Rains* is now in the NLI; and an annotated and revised offprint of the same is extant in private hands, as are other materials. The stages of revision, in which author and translator collaborated, are described by Roger Little ''Saint-John Perse and Denis Devlin: A *Compagnonnage'' Irish University Review* (Dublin) VIII:2 (Autumn 1978) 193-200. The latest, 1962 Pantheon text incorporates the latest revisions, and is the one reprinted here.

Allen Tate recommended the translations to Perse in very strong terms: ''Some days ago Denis sent me his translation of *Pluies* which I hope pleases you as much as it does me. It seems to me from every point of view one of the very finest modern translations from the French. It is a fine English poem, and it seems to me to achieve this quality with very little sacrifice of literal meaning'' (letter dated 24 July 1944; cited by Little 195). Tate was at the time Consultant in Poetry at the Library of Congress (as well as by then Editor of *The Sewanee Review*), where Perse had been a Fellow since 1941. Reviews of the 1949 volume include Katherine G. Chapin ''Syntax of the Lightning'' *Voices* (Vinalhaven, Maine) No. 139 (1949) 46-50; and Dorothy Van Ghent ''The Poet as Exile'' *The Western Review* (Iowa City) XIV:3 (Spring 1950) 232-3; and of the 1953 volume, Henri Peyre *Shenandoah* (Lexington, Va) V:1 (Winter 1953) 75-9. I might add that the reservations I express in the Introduction are not widely shared.

LATER POEMS

BC records that DD had in mind a collection which would gather together the poems he had been working on after he left America (*CP* xvi; compare ''Of Denis Devlin'' 5). However, no scheme for such a collection is to be found among his papers, and it can only be deduced. The following poems, several of which are longer and separately more ambitious than any he had written before, would undoubtedly have been central. However, such were DD's habits of composition, that, even though all of them were published in his lifetime, his interest in them continued beyond their first publication and none of them can be confidently considered as being in a finished state.

Also, the poems in this section ideally require the kind of attention Brian Coffey has given to *The Heavenly Foreigner.* Poems like *The Tomb of Michael Collins* properly require a preliminary editing-task which would sift and collate the materials, and show how the final version evolved. Other poems - specifically *The Colours of Love, The Passion of Christ* and *Memoirs of a Turcoman Diplomat* - deserve to be presented in a way which makes available the parts which were not in the end included in the published version. All that can be attempted here is a sketch of the materials involved.

Finally, while BC correctly says that a number of late MSS are fit for publication (*CP* xvi; compare *SP* 12-3), the situation is in fact less clear. The MSS and TSS in the NLI are sorted according to title, in a convenient way, but a considerable amount of work needs to be done to establish their order and separate authority. As I observed in the Preface, the selections published in *SP, CP* and elsewhere are somewhat at random. It is to be hoped that the situation will be remedied before long.

The following reviews are concerned largely with these late poems and their relation to the earlier. Besides the Preface by Allen Tate and Robert Penn Warren to their edition of *Selected Poems* (New York: Holt, Rinehart and Winston, 1963) 9-14, see Ray Smith *Library Journal* (New York) I:15 (15 January 1963) 225; Anon *The Booklist and Subscription Books Bulletin* (Washington, DC) LIX:13 (1 March 1963) 550; Marius Bewley "Poetry and Fashion" *Partisan Review* (New York) XXX:2 (Summer 1963) 306-12 (with another); Stephen Stephanchev "Diplomat's Devotionals" *New York Herald Tribune Book Review* XL:2 (11 August 1963) 7; Hayden Carruth "Silent Voices" *Poetry* (Chicago) CIII:3 (December 1963) 191-2; Howard Moss "The Selected Devlin" *The Sewanee Review* (Sewanee, Tenn) LXXII (1964) 151-6. For reviews of *CP,* see Brendan Kennelly *Dublin Magazine* N.S. IV:1 (Spring 1965) 83-4; Anon "Home and Away" *Times Literary Supplement* 29 April 1965, p.327; Derek Parker "Ariel, Indeed" *Poetry Review* (London) LVI (Summer 1965) 118-20 (with others); Robin Skelton "Britannia's Muse Revisited" *The Massachusetts Review* (Amherst, Mass) VI:4 (Autumn 1965) 829-39 (835-6 esp.); John Rees Moore "Now Yeats has Gone: Three Irish Poets" *The Hollins Critic* (Hollins, Va) III:2 (April 1966) 6-12 (with others).

The Heavenly Foreigner (no. 88) 260

The NLI materials are extensive. They comprise MSS, TSS and corrected TSS and proofs, in pen and ink, and verse and prose, from all stages of DD's life. The majority are brought together in one file, but others are to be found in the file headed *Beata,* and elsewhere. Corrected pages of the *PI* version (see below) are held in the Archives Department of University

College Dublin (catalogue number LA 17)

Successive extracts and versions of the poem were published in the following journals: *Irish Writing* (Cork) No. 8 (July 1949) 43-4; *Envoy* (Dublin) I:4 (March 1950) 23-4; *PI; Inventario degli oggetti d'arte d'Italio* (Florence) March 1950, pp. 34-59 (with a facing Italian translation by Tommaso Giglio); *The Sewanee Review* (Sewanee, Tenn) LVIII:4 (October 1950) 619-31; *World Review* (London) N.S. No. 27 (May 1951) 20-8; *The Belvederian* (Dublin) XVIII:3 (1960) 69-78. The present text is taken from the edition by Brian Coffey (Dublin: Dolmen Editions, 1967), which includes a full discussion of variants and related fragments, which are collated with the most improved version; also an introduction to the personal and literary background of the poem.

BC's edition was reviewed by Basil Payne *Studies* (Dublin) LVII (1968) 104-8 (with others).

The Colours of Love (no. 89).. 275

The MS beginnings of the poem are separately drafted on small leaves, with such titles as *Stanzas, Outside the Sun, Elegy of All Times,* or untitled, afterwards marked in crayon ''C of L''. Not all these separate poems were used, and those that were used were revised, and other separate unused fragments are to be found in other NLI files. The next stage appears to have been the making of TS versions and other TS drafts of individual sections on the same small-sized paper, with revisions and often place-titles added, such as *Parnasilla, Circo Massimo, The Palatine, Villa on the Lake, Evian,* etc. Another clutch of notes on larger paper, and unused drafts, suggests the beginnings of the poem were quite early and overlap *The Heavenly Foreigner.* Then follow separate TS versions of the whole poem on larger paper, with corrections and with extra corrected TS versions of different parts supervening. The poem was first published in *Botteghe Oscure* (Rome) X (1952) 179-85 - the version given here. Four separate parts were reprinted in *The Oxford Book of Irish Verse* ed Donagh MacDonagh and Lennox Robinson (Oxford: Clarendon Press, 1958) 297-8.

Mr. Allen (no. 90).. 281

The first, heavily-revised MS draft was headed (*Violin Teacher* del.) *Mr. Allen;* and the second, *Mr Allen | to my father.* Four successive TSS, equally heavily revised, are followed by a corrected TS and carbon. Though parts of the poem were extensively reworked, its overall shape was complete from the first. The final TS is annotated ''Published in *Irish Times* and *Partisan Review*''. I have not traced the poem in *The Irish Times.* It was published in *Partisan Review* (New York) XXII:3 (Summer 1955) 351-2 (the text given here); and again in *The Spectator* (London) No.6879 (29 April 1960) 617 (which differs in punctuation and in substituting *of* for *in,* in line 21).

For an exploration of early memories in prose, see *Childhood in Ayrshire* in *Poetry Ireland* (N.S. Dublin) No. 2 (Spring 1963) 75-6 (the corrected holograph of which is annotated "Denis' last poem").

The Tomb of Michael Collins (no. 91).. 283

One of the two? earliest MS versions, on University Club, Washington paper, is in seven four-line stanzas. Headed simply *Michael Collins,* it is more negative and satirical of the life that Collins transcended (mean politics, gain, getting and spending). The other, on yellow paper, with the same title and in similar long lines, is again very different from the poem as it developed. There are also related fragments, and related lines headed simply *M.C.*

The first version of the poem as it developed is a MS corrected in pen, pencil and ballpoint, on separate pages, headed successively: *Funeral Ode on the Death of Michael Collins, Triumphal Memorial of the Death of Michael Collins,* (*Memorial* del.) *Ceremonial of the Hero, Michael Collins.* It contains stanzas which were omitted from the final version. One heavily-revised TS is dedicated to Robert Penn Warren (deleted); another, *To my Father;* yet another has *To Ignazio Silone* inserted. There are ten TSS in all, several heavily revised, others corrected more lightly.

One TS is annotated: "Pub. in *Irish Times* & given to *Sew Review.*" I have not traced the poem in *The Irish Times,* but the poem was published in *The Sewanee Review* (Sewanee, Tenn) LXIV:4 (October 1956) 597-9 - the version given here. It was reprinted without change in *The Oxford Book of Irish Verse* ed Donagh MacDonagh and Lennox Robinson (Oxford: Clarendon Press, 1958) 295-6. DD wrote to BC: "The popularesco repetitions 'It is . . .' 'It was . . .' come, deliberately, from the Irish ballad, my aim being to make a ceremonial ode with country ballad elements" (*CP* xix).

Ignazio Silone (1900-78), to whom the poem is dedicated, was a novelist, political activist and militant writer. His memories of Devlin were published in Rome in *Éire Ireland. Weekly Bulletin of the Department of External Affairs* No. 493 (5 September 1960) 4. -

The Passion of Christ (no. 92).. 286

The extensive MS and TS beginnings of the poem are on small notepaper and clearly were written on many occasions, over a period of time. Many of them are separately headed, in German and in English, and many were not included in the final version: for example, *Die Grablegung, Die Kreuzabnehme, Die Höllenfahrt Christi, Die Beweinung Christi,* and *Walking on the Water, The Roman Tribune, News of Christ's Death, Rome, Christus Redivus.* It would appear that the poem began as a series of meditations on Dürer's series of woodcuts, the *Kleine Passion,* first published in 1511 and available in several reproductions. Compare for instance Karl-Adolphe Knappe (ed) *Dürer. The Complete Engravings, Etchings and Woodcuts* (London: Thames and Hudson, 1965) nos. 254-90. Devlin's poem developed away from its origin; he omitted and added to the Dürer series and changed Dürer's order and interpretations. For example, he began like Dürer, with the Fall and the Expulsion from Paradise, though Dürer ends with the Last Judgement, and added the sections on the Good and Bad Thieves.

Early MSS and TSS are differently headed *The Triumph of Christ, Easter* and *The Passion of Christ.* Some contain more sections than the published version, in a different order; there are separate TSS of individual sections; and most of the TSS are corrected, some heavily. The poem was published in *Encounter* (London) IX:6 (December 1957) 14-8 - the version given here.

Allen Tate (1899-1979), to whom the poem is dedicated, in turn dedicated his sequence of *More Sonnets at Christmas* to DD's memory.

Memoirs of a Turcoman Diplomat (no. 93)... 295

The poem appears to have begun as a series of brief epiphanies, with titles such as *Even the Life Expectancy of Dogs has gone up, View of the Golden Horn, Air France, On the Terrace, Lunch at Ankara, Belgrade, The Dutch Chapel, Old ''Young Turk'', Grey* (*Yellow* del.) *Lemon - Torcello, Greek* (*loves* del.) *Greek.* Among these, *View of the Golden Horn* became the opening lines of the present poem, and *Belgrade* became part of *The White City*; other sections were not used. There is also a continuous MS draft of the poem in its present form, though the separate sections are much revised, and there are two separate corrected TSS. The poem was published in *Botteghe Oscure* (Rome) XXIV (1959) 104-9, the version given here. I offer a commentary on the poem in the essay referred to in the Introduction footnote 14.

UNCOLLECTED LATER POEMS AND TRANSLATIONS

Palm, from Valéry (no. 94)... 304

There are two early MS drafts and a holograph fair copy of the translation. It was published with the original *en face* in *Quarterly Review of Literature* (New Haven, Conn) III:3 (1947) 286-91. Compare *Palme* in Paul Valéry *Œuvres* (Paris: NRF/Gallimard, 1957-60) I 153-6.

Parsifal, from Verlaine (no. 95).. 307

There is a TS of the translation, which was published, following the original, in *The Limits of Art. Poetry and Prose Chosen by Ancient and Modern Critics* ed Huntington Cairns (New York: Pantheon Books, 1948) 1325-6. Compare *Parsifal* in Paul Verlaine *Œuvres poètiques complètes* (Paris: NRF/Gallimard, 1962) 427.

Nineteen Poems by Char, with Jackson Matthews (no. 96).................. 308

The NLI materials suggest that DD was the moving spirit in the translations and it is difficult to fathom the contribution made by Matthews. The lists of what DD had translated or proposed to translate are in his hand, as well as a list of questions for Char (dated 15 July 1952). MS drafts of several poems, and corrections and added titles to several TSS, are in DD's hand. One TS list is headed by him, ''translated by Denis Devlin''; and the twenty-six page continuous TS of the poems as published is among his papers. The translations were published, as ''by Denis Devlin and Jackson Matthews'', with the French original following, in *Botteghe Oscure* (Rome) X (1952) 128-62 (128-46 esp.)

The first eleven poems (up to *To an Image of Warrior Ardour)*, are translated from *Fureur et Mystère* (Paris: Gallimard, 1958); the remainder (from *Flushed with Joy* onwards) are from *Les Matinaux* (Paris: Gallimard, 1950). Cross-references to René Char *Oeuvres complètes* (Paris: NRF/Gallimard, 1983) are as follows:

Wind Away/Congé au vent: Char 130
The Basket-Weaver's Love/La Compagne du vannier: Char 131
Youth/Jeunese: Char 132
Living/Conduite: Char 149
Postscript/Post-scriptum: Char 154
Hymn in a Low Voice/Hymne à voix basse: Char 253
Lily of the Valley/Le Muquet: Char 254
Martha/Marthe: Char 260-7
To the Health of the Serpent/À la santé du serpent: Char 262-7
The Meteor of the 13th of August/Le Météore du 13 août: Char 268-70
To an Image of Warrior Ardour/À une ferveur belliqueuse: Char 277

Flushed With Joy, Those That rise in the Morning/Rougeur des matineaux: Char 329-35
Divergence/Divergence: Char 293
The Advice of the Look-Out/Conseil de la Sentinelle: Char 303
Pyrenees/Pyrénées: Char 304
On Leave/Le Permissionnaire: Char 307
Nights of Fulfillment/Les nuits justes: Char 310
Fully/Pleinement: Char 324-5
Wherefore Yield?/Pourquoi se rendre? Char 335

Wind Away is headed *Farewell Wind* in one TS; the second poem, simply *Weavers*; the fourth poem, *Guidance; Flushed with Joy*, etc, successively *The Early Risers, The Morning Ones* and *Joy of the Forerunners*. DD remarked in his list of questions for Char that he was particularly uncertain about titles and proper names. He also expressed doubts about his translations of *The Advice of the Look-Out* and *Flushed with Joy*.

It appears that DD translated at least three more poems than were published in *Botteghe Oscure* - two from the 1958 volume, one from the 1950 volume -, but there is no trace of these among the NLI materials.

Abel (no. 97).. 329

The first revised draft is headed *The Only Revenge of Abel*. This title is deleted, and a second draft (on Légation d'Irlande Rome paper) is headed *The Sad Revenge of Abel*. There is also a revised TS of the first four lines, untitled, and a TS headed *Abel*.

Dürer's *Kleine Passion* does not include a woodcut of Abel, but the present poem might have grown out of the developing *Passion of Christ* (see no. 92 above). DD chose it as his own contribution to the selection of Irish poets quoted in the Introduction - *New World Writing* (New York) No. 4 (1953) 269.

INDEX OF TITLES AND FIRST LINES

Index of Titles and First Lines